"Brad Larson answers the serious cris[...] serious book. He is clear, he is learned, [...] to restore the loss of valiant manhood [...] should live out the important truths in its pages."

—**Stephen Mansfield**, *New York Times* Bestselling Author

"Follow Brad Larson through *Show Yourself a Man* as he helps reorient the hearts of men in our current cultural topography. In so doing, you may find that Jesus overturns tables in the temple of YOU."

—**Elliott Hillock**, Christ-follower, husband, father, and owner of Freedom Shooting Sports

"I speak at outdoor men's retreats throughout the year, and the topic I address most often is, 'Where did all the men go?' Brad addresses facts about today's men and challenges us to step up and be a man. I will use this book as a reference for many more outdoor men's retreats."

—**Bink Grimes**, author of *Sunrise, Sunset: Devotionals for the Sportsman and Outdoor Enthusiast*, and *Saltwater Strategies: Where, When, and How to Wadefish Texas*; owner of Matagorda Sunrise Lodge and Matagorda Sunrise Properties

"A pervasive softness has found its way into the fabric of today's definition of manhood and it must end. In *Show Yourself a Man*, Brad Larson illuminates the lie and offers a truthful alternative to what really defines manhood."

—**James Trawick**, CEO of Atonement Entertainment

"Brad lays the cornerstone and builds the foundation for structuring a morally sound and well-built life. He accommodates those who need corrections as well as those seeking a path, and ultimately conveys the key concept that a man must lead by faith and example. The Moore family sees our father's stride through these pages and can see Brad's theme lived out in the life our father lived until his passing in February, 2017."

—Family of Lt. Gen. Hal Moore

Show Yourself a Man

BRAD LARSON

End the confusion. Form your identity.
Forge your manhood.

LUCIDBOOKS

To Dad and Liam

Table of Contents

Introduction

Picture this: You are *a man on fire*. You are a fearless, fire-breathing man who runs hard after God. You fight like a savage to push back darkness. You are a man of strength, capability, and wisdom. You endure—no matter what. You are a faithful man who keeps his promises. You are a warrior. You do not run after false gods or dead-end promises; you trust God at his Word. You keep your passions and immature anger in check. You lay down your life for the good of others because you *want to*, as you are motivated by God's work in your heart. You make a ruckus and disrupt your environment—in a good way.

Did I just describe you?

Men are in trouble. We lag behind women four to three in obtaining a college degree.[1] We're increasingly absent in the home. A large swath of working-age men have disappeared from the labor force.[2] Men are almost four times more likely to commit suicide than women.[3] Some studies suggest testosterone levels in men have decreased over the past twenty years.[4] Society tells a man a million different versions of what he should and should not be. Men are understandably confused.

We have been outsourced. We wonder if we're even needed anymore. We can put food on our tables by pressing buttons. We have grown soft and aimless. We wonder as we wander.

The man on fire described above is not you. It's not me, either. The man I described is Jesus, and we fall short of his standard of perfection. I'm not saying we're losers; I am saying we have a long way to go to be like him. Do you long to approach life like Jesus? Do you want to end the confusion, form your identity, and forge your manhood? Do you want to unearth your insecurities and throw them off a cliff? Do you want to look your fears in the face and move toward them? Do you want to put a bullet in the head of your idols?

Good. This book is for you.

Ten years ago I sat with a cup of coffee and two great men—my dad and my uncle—to begin the research for this book. Then I started writing. I trashed several feeble attempts at a rough draft. But the dream of this book would not die. Over the past decade, I have read, studied, and observed the commonalities among strong, godly men. God has richly blessed me with an abundance of outstanding men to learn from, and I have taken notes. *Show Yourself a Man* is my way of sharing what I have learned. I am not the example, but I do hope to be a guide.

Regardless of your age, you are on the road to manhood. It is a journey, not a destination; and the path for a Christian man leads toward a life under the kingship of Jesus. But what does that path look like? Is there any way to look ahead to prepare for the journey? Can we learn anything right here, right now that will help us become strong men living under the kingship of Jesus? I answer these questions and more in this book.

In chapter one, we explore the current state of manhood in our culture. We consider how women perceive men and what society looks like when men lack chests. Relativism has distracted and confused men, and the gender identity movement has made the situation worse. Satan has poured lies on top of lies and told men what they aren't. Spun off course, men have avoided growing up.

Chapter two takes us into the process of growing up. How does a man become a man? He goes through boyhood, adolescence (which I liken to a hormone rocket balloon), and young adulthood. The young man stands at The Precipice, the stage just before becoming a man. As men grow up, they are moldable, and by the time they're adults the world has molded them—but they aren't finished products.

Chapter three examines the various idols men are prone to worship, such as sex, money, and comfort. These idols are misplaced attempts at finding what Jesus offers. Men chase these idols to their detriment, but God is on their tails.

Chapter four leads us into doing the work of forming our identity as men under God's kingship. To do so, we must dethrone ourselves as the center of our world, and we must put God in his rightful place. He is our Father and King. As men, we must decide who we believe Jesus to be. Is he a wise teacher? A prophet? A liar? A character in a fairy tale? Or is he God? Our belief about Jesus will guide our lives and it will determine our eternity. We must then consider who God says *we are*. If we are in Christ, we are sons of God—that's who he says we are. We are his sons! What does that mean for us?

Chapter five takes us deep into the essence of Christian manhood. What does it look like to show yourself a man? God calls the weaklings—regular guys like you and me—to his mission, and he beckons for them to follow. When they do, they are changed into strong, faithful men. When they walk in his ways, they flourish. When they heed his call, they grow.

In chapter six, we open our minds. We men should be learners and explorers of wisdom. Jesus was. Expanding our minds will help us frame the world and ultimately bring us closer in our relationship with God. It will also make us more effective in his service.

Chapter seven addresses an often overlooked topic: a man's body. A man should be as strong and healthy as possible. He is a dwelling place of the Spirit, and thus he should work to make himself strong and durable. Living in a broken world, our bodies will break down; but it is incumbent upon us to build our bodies up as best as we are able.

In chapter eight, we turn the focus to the hearts of men. Getting outside is not just for outdoorsmen; it is for all men. Nature stirs us to worship, as it reveals the glory of God. In addition to enjoying the outdoors, men should also pursue the magical world of art and creativity. Art engages the heart and brings the depth of a man's soul to the surface. It is manly to pursue art. Nature and art help us to be present. They bring us down from the clouds and into the here and now. To stoke our hearts, we need to be present—much like when we were boys. Our boyhood zest for life is not dead; we just need to unearth it.

Chapter nine explores the idea of the gentleman savage. He is a peaceful warrior who is capable of combat but chooses peace. If needed, he can speak the language of violence, but he chooses to do so only in extreme situations and out of love. Jesus was the lion and the lamb, a juxtaposition of ferocity and tenderness. As men we should seek this balance.

In chapter ten, we conspire to disrupt the world. Jesus was a disrupter; his life changed the course of history. As we follow Jesus and claim his name, we will disrupt others. As we seek to love like Jesus loved, we will confuse people. Their curiosity might lead them to ask the eternal questions, and this is a good thing. We should seek to build disruptive organizations as well, from churches to businesses to our family units.

We consider in chapter eleven what it takes to endure the long race of life. Running hard after God is a long game in which we can become tired. We need to fuel up on his grace and rest along the way. We need to understand we'll be tired often if we're living right, and we need to learn to man up and persevere. With our eyes on the prize of heaven—deep intimacy with Christ—we can run ahead with endurance.

Finally in chapter twelve, we look down the road to the end of our journey. A man should run hard to the end and die used up and scarred—with a smile on his face. He should build a legacy that tells a beautiful story for those who come after him. He should live hard—and die hard.

Let me be clear: this book is not the Bible. It is subservient to the Bible. If I have been faithful to my goal, the truths contained herein are all rooted in biblical truth. Assuming that's the case, the truths found in *Show Yourself a Man* are based on God's truth. (If not, throw this book out.) My prayer is that this book is a restatement of God's truth about manhood, because we badly need God's perspective rather than one man's opinions or anecdotes.

Men are down, but not out. We don't need to file masculine bankruptcy. Our churches, homes, and communities need us to be the men God has called us to be. We just need to get our hands dirty. This book is a call for men everywhere: rise up, and show yourself a man.

Let us begin the journey.

Aimless Male Bipeds

We make men without chests and expect from them virtue and
enterprise. We laugh at honor and are shocked to find traitors in
our midst.

—C.S. Lewis, *The Abolition of Man*

Men, we are in big trouble.

The male gender is in bad shape. The world doesn't expect much from us anymore. Because we have broken promises, given way to cowardice, and lived half-heartedly, we have conditioned the world to lower its expectations of us. It's not just women who have noticed this decline of men; our kids and fellow men have also lowered the bar as we have repeatedly tripped over it. We have overpromised and underdelivered. We have failed to be the men God has called us to be.

We once farmed, but now massive corporations do that. We once hunted for our food, but now we drive through. We once fought with our fists, but now we use our keyboards. The postmodern world is not sure what to do with men, and men aren't sure what to do with the postmodern world. It's like that game where you put your head on a bat and spin around ten times and then run. It's no surprise we stumble and fall over sideways.

Men have been outsourced, and we don't know what to do with ourselves. We are soldiers without a war, doctors without patients, and teachers with no students. We are all dressed up with nowhere to go. We want something to apply our strength against, but in today's world many of us find very little worth fighting for.

Earlier today I took my kids to the park. A dog wandered up to us. It had no tag. Our neighborhood has a Facebook page, so I posted a picture to let the owner know where to find the dog. Later I checked my post to see if the owner had responded. Meanwhile, another thread had popped up. A man in our neighborhood was ranting about how slow people drive from our town to the next. Several people dogpiled on and joined the rant. Most of them were men. A woman—a voice of reason—mentioned that maybe some drivers are elderly or just learning to drive. The keyboard ninjas attacked her.

Like I said, we're in serious trouble.

While all men seem confused, men in the lower and middle classes are being hit hard. In her *New York Times* article entitled "A Woman's Place," Jennifer Homans writes (referring to Hanna Rosin's book *The End of Men*):

> But this "rise," which Rosin so cheerfully reports, is in fact a devastating social collapse. It starts with inequality and class division. As Rosin herself shows, men at "the top" of society are not "ending." It is all happening to the lower and middle classes, because "the end of men" is the end of a manufacturing-based economy and the men who worked there, many of whom are now unemployed, depressed, increasingly dependent on the state and women to support them.[1]

The information economy has changed the game for men, and they are struggling to keep up. I'd argue, by the way, that men are struggling in all socioeconomic classes.

The problem of men is not merely frustrating; the ramifications are huge. When men flounder, societies flounder. Families crumble. Poverty rises. Crime increases. When men aren't men, everyone suffers.

The steel-spined men of the Greatest Generation are nearly gone. Now their kids, the Baby Boomers, are the geriatric majority. Generation X isn't too far behind. The men of the Greatest Generation weren't a perfect generation. Let's not paint a rainbow and forget plenty of men from this era were racists and emotionally absent from their families. Monsters lived in their ranks just as in all generations since Adam. But the moral agreements they made as a generation of men were solid: hard work, community, and family. More important to note was the existence of acceptable moral agreements to live by.

Relativism has made the world light-headed. The Trojan Horse of tolerance has brought with it the tenets of moral and spiritual relativism. Relativism claims that truth is relative, not fixed. Each person determines individual truth. Moral relativism holds that what is right for me is right for me, and what is right for you is right for you ("do what you want in your own house"). While this trend has reduced discrimination against many people, which is to be celebrated, it has also confused men. When morality is relative, virtue is relative. If virtue itself is relative, masculine virtue is also relative. Men no longer know who they should strive to be. They don't know whether to even bother striving.

Relativism is on the rise. According to Barna researchers, 57 percent of American adults believe knowing right and wrong is based on personal experience. Seventy-four percent of millennials agree with the following statement: "Whatever is right for your life or works best for you is the only truth you can know."[2]

Here is the problem with this kind of thinking: relativism takes a stand against taking a stand, unless you're taking a stand against those who take a stand. Confused? You should be.

Relativism is bad for both genders, but this shifting foundation is bad for men in particular. Relativism strips away conviction, as the firm adherence to an absolute moral truth is a cultural taboo. Part of owning our manhood includes owning our convictions, those tightly held beliefs that are worth defending. A man's conviction should compel him, whether he storms the beaches of Normandy or fights for civil rights.

But we cannot blame relativism.

Technology has also emasculated men. We are apex predators, the managers of the earth. Yet go to a crowded public place and look at us. I'm not just talking about our physical appearance (we will get to that). I am talking about the ridiculousness of a powerful being made in the image of God slumped over, staring at a rectangle with a glass screen. Our shoulders hunch, our heads stoop, and our fingers cradle these devices like Gollum protecting "precious," the ring in *Lord of the Rings*. According to Deloitte, Americans check their phones an average of forty-six times per day. This is an impediment to deep thought and situational awareness. It distracts men from being where they are and leads them into a portal of where they would like to be.

But we cannot blame technology.

As men are falling behind, women are running ahead. Women are more educated and powerful than ever. Though some work still needs to be done regarding equal pay for equal work, women are leaping forward professionally. As women are rising, men are declining. Feminism seems to have done a good job of advocating for women, but the plight of women has been very different from the plight of men. While women dealt with marginalization—for example, fighting for the right to vote until 1920—men have mostly brought the decline upon themselves. We need advocacy for men; however, it will be of a different flavor, and it must not put us in competition with women. In fact, we should celebrate our sisters as they rise.

Because the problem isn't women.

Many factors converge into the malaise of males, but the world is not to blame. It's easy to point our finger at culture or technology. We can blame video games or diet or the economy even, but these external factors are symptoms, not causes.

The problem with men is men.

DISMEMBERED GENDER

The struggle of men has caused culture to try to redefine the male gender. The definitions are schizophrenic. Our society asserts that the old definitions seem arcane, and even if they aren't, they are at least irrelevant because we live in a new world. The old notions of manhood don't work in today's world, or so the story goes. Consider male characters in movies: the vulgar but witty fat guy, the mysterious double agent, a weepy but powerful vampire, and the superhero, just to name a few. These one-dimensional characters portray a caricature of some aspect of culture's estimation of masculinity. But in no way do they tell a true story of what a man is.

Manhood is deeper and more complex than this.

Beyond the entertainment industry's various definitions of men is the gender identity movement. This movement is aimed at redefining gender as fluid, a choice each individual makes as to whether they want to be a man or a woman. This movement is a step toward chaos and confusion as we move away from the natural, God-given definitions of gender.

Planned Parenthood's website puts it this way:

> *What does it mean to be a woman or a man? Whether we are women or men is not determined just by our sex organs. Our gender includes a complex mix of beliefs, behaviors, and characteristics. How do you act, talk, and behave like a woman or man? Are you feminine or masculine, both, or neither? These are questions that help us get to the core of our gender and gender identity.*[3]

Do you see how the lines are blurred? A male who has distinctly feminine qualities is not a woman; rather, he is a male with female qualities. You cannot think yourself into a different gender. It's a done deal from birth, and even advanced surgical procedures cannot fully transform one's gender.

No main vein of masculine identity exists in our culture. In fact, the only cultural agreement is that there is no universal masculine identity to strive toward (that's relativism).

Clear gender identity is a good thing. The infinitely wise Creator made the world to function in a certain way. When we live within the boundaries of his intended design, we flourish. God designed gender with great intention and purpose. He designed the two sexes beautifully in their own way, and their contrast is part of what makes it all work.

Regarding marriage, Paul Tripp says it this way:

> One way God establishes beauty is by putting things that are different next to each other. Isn't this exactly what God does in marriage? He puts very different people next to each other. This is how he establishes the beauty of a marriage. The moon would not be so striking if it hung in a white sky; in the same way, the striking beauty of a marriage is when two very different people learn to celebrate and benefit from their differences and to be protected from their weaknesses by being sheltered by the other's strength.[4]

The contrast in marriage does not exist only on the basis that each person is a unique creation. While this is true, the contrast in marriage is beautified by gender. Men and women are complementary to one another, and healthy marriages reflect this God-intended juxtaposition.

Our gender helps frame our path in life. As we look at the world around us and decide how we will respond, our gender helps inform our choices. It is a defining part of who we are. The gender identity movement has gained such traction because everyone agrees gender is important.

We know this intuitively, but we still want to be God. We come out of the womb gendered by our Creator, but many want to change their gender after the fact. This is a quest for power, not a means of self-expression. And it is a road to heartbreak.

God is not sorry he made you a man. You are not defective or partially made. Maybe you are not the cookie-cutter version of a manly man. That is okay. God will build your manhood in a unique way if you are willing. It's not machismo that makes us a man. What matters is to accept and embrace the fact that you are indeed a man.

RAZORBLADE CANDY

When I was growing up, people warned kids to look for razors or needles in their Halloween candy. Though I am sure this was an old wives' tale and few kids actually bit into candy booby traps, it made everyone think twice. It made some moms frantic with fear; thus, a lot of kids didn't get to eat their Halloween candy.

As you pursue your masculinity, the Devil wants you to think razors are in your candy. He wants you to be scared, confused, and skeptical. He badly wants to undermine your masculinity. He wants you to believe his lies. These lies lead away from faithfulness and toward death and disaster. Have you ever heard any of the following?

- You aren't a real man.
- God is not king, you are.
- Don't tell her that—it's corny.
- No one will know.
- You're blowing it.

Here's the thing. These razor-blade candy lies taste sweet in the moment. They seem to ring true. And these lies may indeed seem sweet after you act upon them, but sooner or later you will realize their power is based on evil. Your thinking has become twisted, and as you feed on razor-blade candy lies, you get a mouth full of blood.

The best way to manipulate a man is to tell him a story. Stories frame our lives, and if we are to live well, we must live within the right story. The Devil has honed his storytelling skills over thousands of years, and he asks you to pull up a chair and sit a spell. He is cunning, and many a man has been destroyed by his false stories.

We can't go around blaming the Devil for our lost manhood. There is no need to fear him. He's a disgusting deceiver, but for those of us who are in Christ, he has no power over us unless we buy into his pitch. We must be aware of his lies.

DELAYED MANHOOD

According to the BBC, over 250,000 underage men finagled their way into the British military to fight in World War I.[5] These boys lied about their age to get into the fight. It was common for young men to lie about their age or get around a physical defect so they could join the military. Rudyard Kipling's son was among them.[6] Due to his poor eyesight, he used his father's connections to get into the infantry. Rudyard Kipling wrote his famous poem "If" to his son, Lt. John Kipling. Like millions of others, John died in the war. He was last seen staggering around, covered in mud and blood.

These boys were a different breed of teenager from those we know today, lying their way into a war that claimed the lives of more than 16 million people.[7] Before their beards came in, these boys shot the enemy and held their friends as they watched them die. In World War I, these young men endured horrible conditions: shelling, frostbite, gassing, and hunger. I am not saying this is a good thing, but this attitude and behavior is mostly foreign to today's teenagers. You could say that these boys rushed into manhood.

It is hard to picture enduring what these brave boys went through, but it is even harder to picture the teenage boys of today volunteering for this kind of fight. It is a different world, and our teens—well, many of them—know very little about duty and sacrifice.

Today the goal seems to be to delay male adulthood.

Men are getting married later. Some say they want to get on their feet with a stable job before considering marriage. Some say they'd like to travel first. For many young men, these excuses are just a smokescreen to hide the fact that they don't want to grow up.

According to the findings of the National Marriage Project at Rutgers University:

> *The researchers note that most people think it's men, not women, who are "dragging their feet about marriage," and they state "our investigation of male attitudes indicates that there is evidence to support this popular view." The primary reason given by men for taking their sweet time: They can get sex without marriage more easily now than in the past.*[8]

This attitude is indicative of the state of our men. They want to bed women, not marry them. And apparently many women are okay with this.

Women are far too easy on men, and their standards are far too low. When a daughter of God accepts a half-man as a husband, she validates him. She hands him the key to her majestic heart. It would be better for everyone if women would up their standards. I do have to grant my sisters this, however: the options are few. There are plenty of honorable, godly men out there, but the percentages are discouragingly low. Worse for women is that popular culture tells them that they should be rail thin, beautiful, and sexually liberated. Many women feel pressure to meet this stereotype, and those who do tend to live with broken hearts. Too often, men reinforce these stereotypes. Ultimately, it is women who pay the debt for the delayed manhood of men.

I met my wife, Lindsay, in my freshman year in college. We had moved in next door to each other in a private dorm at Texas A&M University. I met her in the hall as we carried our boxes to our rooms on moving-in day. Shortly after getting settled in, my roommates and I made friends with a group of guys down the hall. We found a shared pastime: drinking cheap whiskey in large quantities. We'd often get drunk and carry on until the wee hours. While her neighbors were cranking music and getting good at making bad decisions, Lindsay was next door struggling to get used to being away from her family. She was a stark contrast to me and my buddies: sober, sweet, and pretty.

I was interested in Lindsay from the moment I saw her. So first chance I got, I asked her if she wanted to go out. She said no. But I did not give up so easily. I asked her out again and again until she said yes. Our first date was to Chick-fil-A with a stop at the cleaners to pick up my clothes. I had forgotten my wallet so she paid for everything.

Thank God for her low standards.

Over the next several years, as we dated and eventually became engaged, God sanctified me through Lindsay. While she did lower her bar for me initially, she actually had high standards, and her high standards—along with her love—helped move me toward the Lord and away from my sin. This was not my goal, nor was it hers. By God's grace it happened, and we grew together spiritually. I am deeply grateful for her.

I was a 23-year-old boy when we got married. Of course, God knows what he's doing, but looking back it seems that giving me Lindsay's hand was like giving a deranged chimp a samurai sword and a fifth of Jack Daniels. Damage was inevitable.

Many young men delay maturity like I did. They party through high school and college. They waste valuable years. They delay their true manhood by living a parody of manhood. I know. I have been there.

It doesn't have to be this way.

FREEDOM THROUGH RESPONSIBILITY

Men, we are infected with the disease of aimlessness. This is an easily curable disease. But if we don't cure it, we'll be aimless male bipeds—apex predators staggering through life with no direction. God has a rewarding mission for men, but aimlessness causes mission drift.

An aimless man—one without purpose and direction—will generally choose no direction at all. He will have paralysis by analysis.

What has caused this aimlessness? It is primarily our affluence, which has given us an overabundance of choices in life, e.g., what to do with our lives. No longer do we grow up on a farm and thus become farmers, or grow up in the house of a blacksmith and thus become a blacksmith. We can go to college online or in person. We can start a business, or we can study to be a lawyer. We can be a preacher or a scientist. All information is at our fingertips. Endless entertainment is, too. This abundance of choices tends to produce aimlessness.

In 1966, Alfred E. Kahn wrote the article "The Tyranny of Small Decisions," which states the results of his study on the economic effects of numerous small transactions. Kahn argues that the combination of many small transactions made by rational consumers can eventually be detrimental.[9] The abundance of little decisions by consumers, though rational on the basis of each transaction, can lead to market failure because consumers decide narrowly about each transaction. The larger picture is not in view, so the consumer makes the best decision without understanding the ramifications of their decisions.

Isn't that what we're dealing with as men? Though it goes far beyond our economic choices, each day we make a thousand small decisions: What pants do I wear? Where do I find coffee? Should I check my email right now? And so on. We operate with our heads down, and while each of the many daily decisions we make seems rational, we lose sight of the big picture of our lives. We ignore the big, important questions: Who am I? Why am I here? What really matters? We're too busy deciding what we'll have for lunch. Our abundance of choice keeps us distracted, and the human brain was not designed to function while distracted. Further, our small choices contribute to the larger story of our lives, and if we don't see the canvas on which we're painting, we'll paint something ugly, disjointed, and purposeless. We could be lemmings headed for a cliff. The details of our lives, no matter how mundane, create our story.

The tyranny of small decisions in our lives can create aimless men, and aimlessness wreaks havoc on the hearts of men. We need the larger picture to be in view. Men need a mission.

John Eldredge says,

[I]n the heart of every man is a desperate desire for a battle to fight, an adventure to live, and a beauty to rescue.[10]

These three missions (a battle to fight, an adventure to live, and a beauty to rescue) are not the only missions of manhood, but they are important ones. A man needs something to strive for that is bigger than himself. A mission gives our lives boundaries as to what we will do and what we will not do. It sets us on a path to meaning.

I once had an aimless young man tell me he was an outlaw. We stood around a campfire staring into the flames, as men like to do. He'd had quite a bit to drink, so he swayed as he stood. Through a forced Southern drawl, he blurted that he was an outlaw. We both knew he wasn't; he was a good kid who was incredibly confused. He'd had few boundaries in his life, and the small (and immaterial) decisions of his life overwhelmed him so that he did not see the bigger picture. He longed for identity, but he was stuck in confusion.

The cure for aimlessness is purpose. Purpose typically comes hand in hand with responsibility. For example, when my first child was born, I became responsible to be a father to him. Those with kids know that parenthood is a heavy responsibility. Yet it gave my life great purpose, forcing me to see life through a wider lens. The purpose of fatherhood helped me decide what was worth giving up. To love a child, you must forego sleep, hobbies, and money. It typically affects your sex life with your wife. But it is worth it. The responsibility brings purpose, which brings order to life.

God is a God of order. He designed men in certain ways, and he intended them to be responsible for certain things. When God made Adam and Eve, he gave them dominion over the earth, meaning he tasked them with looking after all the things he'd made. This was a great responsibility, and God knew this was healthy for Adam and Eve. Before sin entered the world, Adam and Eve worked in the garden; they had responsibilities, which was God's design.

When men remain unmarried, they (usually) also delay becoming fathers. Fatherhood and becoming a husband are two daunting responsibilities, and they are two forging fires of manhood. They chip away at selfishness and encourage service to others. They are also the two most rewarding aspects of manhood. Yet many men avoid marriage and fatherhood. We don't need condemnation for delaying responsibility; rather, we need to know the benefits of responsibility. Responsibility strengthens the man. It purifies him. It kills off part of his selfishness and trains him to focus on others.

As a sidebar, it is crucial to mention that singleness is a valid and noble path as well. Paul was single, as was Jesus. Godly singleness is not only admirable, it is helpful to the world. But, as Paul says, most men aren't cut out for it. Most men cannot contain their passions. Most men, myself included, are like Adam: better not left alone.

Regarding taking responsibility seriously, Christian culture has overreacted. For far too long, Christian men have been told to marry early, have kids, work hard, and mow their yards. It's the *Leave It to Beaver* type of life. Now this is actually great advice for most men, and I happen to have a very happy life just like this, but it isn't the gospel. If we imply that a certain domestic lifestyle is the one-size-fits-all for-mula for men, we deceive ourselves. Men do not have to be married to be men. It isn't commanded that they have kids.

They just need to be men.

We all feel aimlessness sometimes, but there is a better way forward: a way of great purpose and responsibility. We must move through the fog of confusion and see God's plan for us as men so we can start to live a great story.

Let's take a look at how we grow into male adulthood. We will examine the phases of growing up so we can figure out just how we got where we are.

CHAPTER 2

Growing Up

Boys are beyond the range of anybody's sure understanding,
at least when they are between the ages of 18 months
and 90 years.

—James Thurber

When I was a young boy, I was afraid I might be gay. I wasn't even sure what being gay meant, but after watching *Real World* on MTV, I realized that some men are gay. I thought I might be one of them, and it scared me.

I remember sweating in homophobic fear. I did not grow up in a fundamentalist household. Far from it—my parents were kind and supportive. They never said a word about homosexuality. Yet somehow I thought that being gay was something I didn't want to be, and I was afraid I was.

It was an identity crisis. I started observing other men to help me figure out who I was. I watched my dad and his friends. They were manly men whom I wanted to be like. Looking back on my brief stage of homophobia, I can see that my fear had nothing to do with being gay. Because I didn't know what that truly meant, I used homosexuality to define what I was scared of.

I was scared of not becoming a man.

The fear of becoming something we don't want to be, or not measuring up to what we long to be, lies within all of us. If we're adults, we may fear that we still aren't the men we should be. When we're young, we worry we might never become who we want to be.

As we grow up, the ingredients of our masculine identity are tossed into a pot: hormones, family life, media, genetics, church, etc. Thus, each man is unique, a concoction of different ingredients influenced by the heat of life. Some men are blessed to have strong ingredients, while others must work with the little they've been given. The ingredient all men must reckon with is some type of fear. It could be fear of failure, or fear of being exposed. Maybe the fear is rational and maybe it isn't, but we all are scared of something.

Fear is a catalyst. It can stimulate good or bad movement in our lives. It can generate life change if we lean into it. While it is important to face our fears in order to conquer them, this is not the most important benefit of facing your fears. Facing your fears as a man will help to identify who you are. What you fear reveals a lot about you, and if you can face those fears that threaten to misidentify you, you will emerge confidently knowing who you are.

The other day my son dropped a toy underneath his bed. He asked me to get it for him because he was scared spiders were under there. Of course, there weren't any spiders, but he thought there were. I reassured him he had nothing to worry about and told him to get the toy himself. *Look, no spiders.* He sat paralyzed on the edge of the bed as I encouraged him to get in there and face his fear. It was a standoff.

"Do you think your daddy would send you under your bed if spiders were there?"

"Well, no." He sniffled.

"Get in there, buddy. It's no big deal. Grab that toy. There's nothing there. I promise."

He cautiously reached in and picked up the toy from underneath the bed. He looked at me. I could see he was holding back a smile.

Just as God sometimes uses suffering to shape us, he also uses fear. He specifically uses fear in building men. It's part of our growing up to deal with fear. It is what drives boys to climb trees and teenagers to race their cars. Facing fear can be fun.

As we grow up, we must conquer our fears or we will become a slave to them. We go through rites of passage when we must push through our fear. We try out for the football team, ask a girl out, and give a presentation to the class. Maybe we stand up to a bully. Staring into the eyes of fear will help forge a man. Looking the other way will weaken him.

Our childhood years make us into who we are as young adults. Watching our fathers and the other men in our lives sets in motion how we form our idea of what a man should be like. This can be either a good thing or a bad thing, depending on the quality of men around us. I played baseball with a kid whose dad beat him with a PVC pipe. It so badly affected this young boy that he developed a slouched posture. He walked looking at the ground, and his eyes darted here and there, like an animal scanning for danger. His dad taught him what a violent scumbag looks like. He showed him a perverse version of manhood. That beaten boy is now a man, though I've lost track of him. I hope Jesus has grabbed hold of him and tended to his wounds. I hope Jesus has showed him what love looks like. I hope he has received the hope of Christ and it has propelled him to become a man very unlike his father.

I can recall a different baseball buddy whose dad showed him unconditional love. As my friend grew up, he followed an example of righteousness. It is no surprise he became a solid man like his father. The men in our lives will shape our understanding of manhood.

Some men have been given the gift of a wonderful childhood, but regardless of how you grew up, you still have the opportunity to be fathered by the Lord. There is grace for us all, and it is never too late.

Let's explore how we got where we currently are in our manhood. To help us, we will review the three primary phases of growing up.

BOYHOOD

Boys will be boys.

My son, Liam, is about to turn six at the time of this writing. He loves bikes, T-ball, drones, and getting dirty. I tell him he's like a wild animal. He doesn't like that very much, but he is. He is a heathen of the best kind. He's my *boy*.

The purest stage of male life is boyhood. Boys are unbridled. Their thoughts, emotions, fears, and joys are on display. Boys are full-hearted. They hide nothing of themselves from the world.

It warms my soul to watch Liam play—and I envy him a little bit. He doesn't care about what he's wearing or what is cool or if his mom and dad are around. He plays with girls and boys just the same. So long as they like bikes and mud and unhealthy food, they're in.

While boys are delightful creatures, the purity of a boy also lets their selfishness out on display. Boys hoard their toys, punch their sisters, and talk back to their parents. The sin in their hearts bubbles up to the surface. It is authentic behavior because they don't yet have the willpower to restrain themselves. What you see is what you get.

Not all boys are rowdy. Some boys are quiet and calm. It is not my intent to promote a stereotype that boys must love mud and bikes, as my son does. In fact, it is important to remember that boys are very tender.

The heart of a boy is a sponge. He takes in the stimuli around him and files it away. Everything he experiences tells him something about himself, especially the way his parents and peers relate to him. As he grows up, his heart collects memories of his boyhood, which will, though perhaps subconsciously, help him become what he is as a man.

My prayer for Liam is that he would be both tough and tender. I pray that he would be strong when he needs to be strong and tender when he needs to be tender. My prayer for myself as his dad is that I will know how to love him as he deserves to be loved.

I once duck hunted with a guide who brought along a yellow Labrador named RJ. Our guide had borrowed RJ from a friend. That morning, we arrived at our spot by a pond before daylight and took our positions in the trees. It was dark, cold, and quiet. Clearly, RJ was excited for the hunt. We all were.

As the eastern horizon lightened with the coming sunrise, the ducks began to fly into the spread of decoys. RJ could withhold himself no longer. His quivering body sprang to action. He plunged into the pond, swimming for the ducks, both decoys and true ducks. To say that our guide was irate is an understatement. A string of obscenities spilled from his mouth, aimed at his buddy's dog. It wasn't enough that he cussed RJ up one side and down the other. With hateful intent, the guide shocked him through his electronic collar, all the while screaming at the swimming dog, who was doing what he was trained to do—albeit a bit out of sync.

What happened is obvious. Our guide had no relationship with RJ. He saw RJ as just a dog—a tool. And dogs should do what they're told. So when RJ didn't listen to our guide, the man took it personally. But RJ had no relationship with our guide, either. The two had no rapport; thus, RJ had no reason to please, or even respond to, someone who wasn't his owner. Given the way our guide was yelling, RJ probably didn't even know what he was being commanded to do.

Many fathers treat their sons the way our guide treated RJ. Sure, it's rarely to that extent, but the principle is the same. When we think boys are tougher than they are, or that they owe us something, we treat them too roughly, like someone else's bird dog. When a grown man wraps his identity around a boy, he asks something of the boy, which the boy cannot handle. It is too much for his young soul. Boys don't need to be coddled, but we must remember they are children, and children are tender.

The boy is a seed of a man, and he is a pure seed. When God waters him and grows him up, he then becomes an adolescent. And whoa! What a wild ride that is.

HORMONE ROCKET BALLOONS

Liam is obsessed with rocket balloons. Rocket balloons are a genius (read: profitable) invention made by repurposing long skinny balloons (the kind used to make balloon animals) and calling them rocket balloons. You fill these balloons with air and then pinch the tip. When you are ready, you release your hold, and the balloon squeals as it shoots into the air in squiggles and circles.

Adolescent boys are like human rocket balloons filled with testosterone. They squeak and squeal as their voices change, and they shoot around in circles because they don't really know what to do with themselves. This is a hard phase of life. For one thing, puberty makes boys capable for sexual experience, but they aren't ready for it. An adolescent boy struggles to do something with his urges, yet he has no proper outlet. He is full of sexual angst.

Adolescence also makes boys gawky and awkward looking. When in this stage of life, I grew tall but my weight remained the same. My legs hurt at night from my body's rapid growth. Then one day it stopped, leaving me gangly, like a baby giraffe.

The adolescent boy—the hormone rocket balloon—has the maturity of a boy but the hormones of a man. He is not physically or emotionally mature. He doesn't know who he is yet, and thus he will often act out to get attention or to test boundaries.

If coddled, he will quickly become weak. He will revert to the childhood he should be passing through. If treated too harshly, he will rebel.

During adolescence, boys form vital aspects of their manhood. Physical abilities in sports emerge. Artistic aptitude grows for some. It is usually during this time that a boy begins to grasp the deeper realities of life. He begins to see the world more clearly, all the while becoming more complex.

At all stages of maturity, it is crucial to saturate boys with the gospel of Jesus Christ. Boys—perhaps especially adolescents—need to taste the grace of Jesus. As they observe and learn about their world, it is important that they see the world through the lens of grace and redemption. When they fail, they need to experience forgiveness and love from their parents and teachers. If they do, they'll be set upon a wise path to grow into men. If they don't, they'll react by finding affirmation wherever they can. The affirmation of God is what really matters. Boys must understand that God displayed his affirmation with the cross of Christ. This is what boys must know—what we all must know.

The adolescent boy is in a painful growing phase in many regards. He is moldable clay in need of grace. And then he becomes a . . . well, not quite.

ALMOST THERE. THE PRECIPICE

I will call this next phase of life The Precipice. The boy is now a young man. He can grow facial hair . . . kind of. He might have developed muscles. His voice is no longer changing. He now stands between childhood and manhood.

But his room might still house his toys in the drawers.

Young men at The Precipice can vote, smoke, drive, move out, and go to war. But they are not quite men. Not yet. War or tragedy might hasten the arrival of manhood at this stage, but most young men at The Precipice are still a distance from fully entering manhood. The foundation of his boyhood and adolescence have shaped him into who he is today, but he is not yet who he will become.

When I was at The Precipice, I tried to speed up the maturation process. I wanted to hurry up and become a man. I got a job and bought some tools. I chewed tobacco and drank and drove a three-quarter-ton truck. Because some of the men I admired at the time chewed, drank, and drove big trucks, I figured if I looked the part, I'd be a man. It was like playing dress up.

There is no way to speed up the process of becoming a man. You cannot fake it. A man is built by God through trials and pain over time. You can aid a young man toward manhood by helping him with his spiritual formation. If he understands who God has called him to be and who Christ already proved he is, he will stand upon solid ground. While not yet mature, he'll be on the path of redemption. The love of Jesus covers us, protects us, and provides for us. The young man needs this knowledge and assurance at the core of his being.

Young men think they know it all. Of course, they don't. It takes time and pain and experience to obtain wisdom.

A young man once told a buddy of mine that he disagreed with the fundamental premise of how we obtain wisdom—that is, over time.

"What do you mean?" my friend asked.

"I just think it's not true that you must obtain wisdom through years of living. I think you can get wisdom from other people. You know, by learning from others."

What he said was partially true but also laughably false. It is common for young men at The Precipice to see life this way. They may have read part of the textbook, but they have not stepped foot into the classroom of life. Of course, wisdom can be obtained by learning from others, but that takes time as well, and true wisdom must be applied and tested over time.

The Precipice is a time of male conquest. Young men at this age want to conquer. They test their strength in many ways, hoping to prove themselves a man. Danger increases at this stage. During this period in my life, I tried drugs and put my truck in a ditch while driving drunk. I made several foolish choices. I was not a boy yet not a man—a boy in a man's body, which is common. Thank God for his grace and protection. He kept me alive, and he worked through my parents to demonstrate discipline and love. He never stopped fathering me; in fact, he still hasn't.

Maturity comes at different speeds for everyone, but at The Precipice we see young men start to gain wisdom of living. The young man might grow in spiritual maturity and understanding, as Jesus did. He may learn how to work, which teaches the value of a dollar. He could lose a family member and drink from the cup of loss. Real life approaches.

As a young man moves through The Precipice, he steps into adult life. This is where the stakes get high.

ETERNAL CLAY SCULPTURES

By the time a boy becomes a young man, he has been shaped by the forces in his life. He has gone through childhood. He has learned that the world is not Eden. Through his choices and the path his life has taken, he becomes what he has experienced. He is a collection of the clay of his past. God, the Potter, is not finished with him yet.

The stakes are high for our men. Shape them properly throughout the younger stages and they will be men full of divine power. Shape them improperly and they'll become Frankensteins of sin. But it is never too late for the rescue of Jesus. It is never too late for you, and it is never too late for the men God has placed in your life. Don't give up on them, and don't give up on yourself. God has given us one another to travel together on the journey of life.

I met Louis on the back porch at a kid's birthday party. We did the friendly head nod and started talking as our kids ate cake. Before I knew it, we were talking about his story—a story of redemption. Jesus rescued Louis from the streets. He pulled him from two drug-dealing parents into the light. Louis had been a drug-dealer as well, and violence and sin marked his former life.

That is, until he met a godly man.

When Louis met a bishop at a church in his hometown, everything changed. Louis did not believe a man could be faithful, but meeting this faithful man challenged his belief. The bishop was faithful to his wife and loving to his community. He drew strength from Jesus and did not put on pretenses. This man introduced Louis to the risen Jesus Christ, and Louis would never be the same. Godly men can change generations.

In his book *Mansfield's Book of Manly Men*, author Stephen Mansfield explains, "All it takes for a contagious manly culture to form is for one genuine man to live out genuine manhood."[1]

Meeting Louis, I encountered a godly and Christ-like man. I met a genuine man living out genuine manhood, who boldly admits his deep need for Jesus. Not long ago, he was a drug dealer. But built by God into a man who builds other men, he is tender with his kids, faithful to his wife, gentle, strong, and confident. It started with Louis meeting that bishop some ten years prior. Now Louis, because of the influence of the godly bishop, has become an ambassador, a representative of what a godly man is.

Being made in God's image, we reflect God to the world. This is a high calling. If we are followers of Christ, we are his ambassadors to the world (2 Cor. 5:20), but we aren't solo ambassadors. This is good, because living out our ambassadorship is too difficult to do alone. We need the company of other ambassadors to encourage us along the way. It is hard growing up. The path of Christian manhood is a hard one. That's why we need allies and comrades as we go through life.

Our allies and comrades—our fellow ambassadors—stand beside us as we grow into the men God wants us to become. It is not easy to understand the trajectory of our lives at any given moment, but as we fight the battles of life alongside our brothers, we will gradually change. Our childhood is part of a story, and God is a storyteller. When we look back on our lives, we will see his hand moving to grow us into men who reflect his glory.

Let us now come to grips with how we try to undermine him.

CHAPTER 3

Idol Machines

*Nothing teaches us about the preciousness of the Creator as much as
when we learn the emptiness of everything else.*
— Charles Haddon Spurgeon,
Morning and Evening

Upon arriving at adult maleness—let's not call it manhood just yet—the man walks onto the battlefield of life. Maybe he lands a job, gets married, and has kids. Maybe he just gets a job. He has less time for nonsense because he has to earn money to pay rent. And if he's working forty hours a week, he has less time for boyhood hobbies and pursuits.

At first, becoming a grown-up is pretty fun. You can eat a bag of Doritos for breakfast if you want. No one tells you when to be home at night, or when to get up in the morning, or how to spend your spare time. You have a little money in your pocket and lots of freedom as to what you do with it. Your life is now in your hands, which is what you've always wanted.

Soon the novelty wears off, though. When the newness wears off, reality sets in. By the time a young man reaches his mid-twenties, he learns being an adult is pretty hard. That bag of Doritos for breakfast proves to be a bad idea. Bills pile up. The job becomes stressful. The young man starts to wonder if he'll find someone to marry or if the girl he's dating is the one. He will question if he's on the right career path. Perhaps he has good men around him (comrades) to provide counsel for his life decisions, but remember he is on his own now. He must figure out the real world on his own.

Of course, not everyone goes through a crisis at twenty-five. Some guys start winning in life right away. They make money doing what they love, marry the girl of their dreams, and take off like a rocket, ticking off their list of goals. Other guys gain twenty pounds and sag into couch cushions while playing video games all night in their parents' basement. Most of us are somewhere in the middle, which is to say, *average*. We aren't losers, but we aren't setting the world on fire, either.

Men don't like to be average. Especially millennials, who grew up hearing how special they are. It's hard to see your snowflakeness melt.

We search for something new and interesting at this point. We start to thrash around. We may pick up mountain biking, change jobs, or develop an interest in politics. Maybe we take a road trip with some buddies. Not satisfied with the drudgery of the real world, we hunt for something worthwhile—or at least something fun. But road trips end, and, despite our searching, we still feel there's a deeper meaning to life we've missed. Once we are well underway on our trip through the real world, we start to panic subconsciously. *Is this all there is?*

Scripture grounds us here: "Only let each person lead the life that the Lord has assigned to him, and to which God has called him" (1 Cor. 7:17).

God has blessed us with certain talents and abilities, as well as an environment within which to use them for the good of other people and the glory of God. Some guys wear white collars, many wear blue collars, while others wear no collars. From birth we are set upon a certain path, and while that path is free and open to us, God knows very much the steps we will take.

But it all seems too mundane. The high school cliques disperse, and we wrinkle and gain twenty or more pounds. We thought we'd be CEOs, musicians, and cowboys . . . but those daring dreams faded when reality intruded. We are mid-level managers, struggling entrepreneurs, and unhappy lawyers. It isn't all bad, it's just so . . . ordinary. We wonder if this is really the life God has assigned to us.

Surely not, we think.

Settled into the groove of adulthood, we begin a search for novelty—that feeling we had when we first stepped into adulthood. Some men search for meaning in their walk with God and find it. Others, even some who have a relationship with Jesus, search for more interesting diversions. Living life with Jesus is an epic adventure, but many don't recognize this. They think Jesus is their homeboy, or an overbearing headmaster, or an absentee landlord who rules from afar. He is none of these. He is our king, savior, and friend. And he is never boring. But if we don't know this, we will search elsewhere.

So we create idols to worship.

SEX

According to Covenant Eyes, the pornography industry generates an annual revenue of over $13 billion. Christian men aren't immune: 64 percent say they look at porn at least once per month.[1] Sex sells and men are buying.

I often leave very early in the morning—before the roosters are up—to attend various meetings. When on the freeway out of the city, I have to pass by a seedy part of town, where several porn shops are located. I cannot help but note the number of cars in the parking lots.

People are always there.

I'm surprised people are awake at all when I roll through town before daylight, but that people—the stats say mostly men—are in porn viewing rooms at this hour is nauseating. I cannot imagine what chains these men must drag around with them: the shame, the addiction, the dark thoughts. I wonder about their wives and children, if they have them.

What I have found by walking with men who struggle with pornography is that most men struggle with shame. They often ignore the damage caused by porn: addiction, desensitization, disruption of marriages and relationships with children, and more. But their shame they cannot disregard. They just don't want to get caught. While having their addiction exposed is certainly bad, it is not the worst aspect of pornography. We must consider the collateral damage.

Porn produces an abundance of victims. Porn producers victimize actors, treating them as objects rather than human beings. They also view the audience as mere things to be manipulated out of their money. Men virtually cheat on their wives and girlfriends, making them unwilling—sometimes unknowing—victims of their addiction. Whether or not you call watching porn infidelity or not, it is certainly not fidelity. And it is harmful to relationships.

While in college, my wife—at the time, girlfriend—found porn on my computer. I will never forget that moment. Sweat immediately beaded all over me. Then the lies popped out. "I must have a virus. Something is wrong with my computer . . ."

She just looked at me like the idiot I was.

Then I remembered sitting in church in the weeks before she discovered my secret. I wore a heating blanket of guilt. I couldn't pay attention to the sermon because all I could think about was the unconfessed sin hidden in my heart. Unconfessed sin burdens us and separates us from our most important relationships, including our relationship with God. It's like a home infested with termites. All looks okay on the surface, but the insides are deteriorating. At some point the house will fall. Whenever the pastor turned his attention anywhere near personal holiness or sexual immorality, I burned with shame.

This was more than a decade ago, and I can say with great thankfulness that I have zero temptation to look at porn. By the grace of God, the thought of it is revolting to me. As God made my sin bitter, Christ became sweeter. Jesus did the work here, not me.

It takes a while for the mental images to go away, but they eventually do. The Lord does not merely forgive the sin; he also cleanses and purifies the memory. Clearly, those who have a long history of sexual immorality have a lot of work to do. They must un-remember many things. No matter if your engagement with sexual sin is short or a lifetime, God is faithful not only to rescue you from your sexual darkness but also to help you regain purity of mind. I won't sugarcoat it; this will be a long, uphill process. It will be hard, but I guarantee that your regained purity will be worth all the hardship. But you must be willing to put in the work, to trust, and to trudge on.

Some men may think they're in the clear because they don't look at porn. But a second look at a woman in the wrong way, a held glance at a sex scene in a movie, or a mental fantasy with anyone other than his wife is no better.

Jesus explains, "But I say to you that everyone who looks at a woman with lustful intent has already committed adultery with her in his heart" (Matt. 5:28).

That's heavy, isn't it? Essentially, the man who looks at other women lustfully is offering his heart in worship to an evil substitute for God's plan. Jesus is after the heart, not the behavior. It isn't about your record of righteousness; it's about intent. And lust is intent to commit adultery. God's standard for sexual purity is a very high standard, which should humble us and cause us to joyfully repent when we violate it. Thankfully, God goes with us and before us. He provides his Word and his Spirit to minister to us.

A newly married man who has viewed porn will find that his sexual expectations are not realistic. They are not grounded in reality because they are built from dark lies about women and intimacy. His wife may not share his preferences or appetite for sex, which isn't exactly a plot that sells adult films. Thus, these naïve men are particularly susceptible to giving in to temptation. They excuse their sin, reasoning that they aren't getting what they think they deserve. By the way, it isn't just young men who fall for this lie and struggle with the idol of sex. Men of all ages are susceptible.

When we *feel* God is not enough, we seek to replace him. If we allow our emotions or carnal desires to drive us, we will seek what we think will fulfill them. When we are not fulfilled with an intimate spiritual relationship with Jesus, we may seek to solve our loneliness through illicit sexual means. In doing so, we forget that what Jesus offers is far superior to any sexual experience. We give in to temptation because we forget the payoff of self-control is wonderful, and it strengthens us. We forget the power of the Spirit to lead us away from temptation.

Don't sell your heart. Don't victimize other people because you're needy. God offers a better way to experience intimacy and joy.

MONEY

Money makes a pretty decent false god . . . at least temporarily. Money is powerful. It can increase your status among your friends and co-workers. Money can take you places and buy you stuff and even bring new friends. That is, until it is exposed as an empty god with no love, no benevolence, and no peace. And as sure as the sun rises in the east, eventually its barrenness of what we truly seek for a good life will be revealed. Money is a lifeless measure of value, and its only power is that which we give to it. Too many people chase after it like a god.

Men can make money their idol whether they have very little or millions of dollars. Those with large bank accounts typically use it to build their kingdoms on earth. They use their god to buy cars, vacation homes, and other goods they value. Likewise, those who live hand-to-mouth elevate money as the answer to their life's problems, so they spend their time and energy seeking it. But money never solves life's problems, for it is an intensifier. It brings out what is already within the heart.

Jesus talked a lot about money because he knew we needed to hear the truth about it. Jesus warned us about the danger of using or viewing money improperly. When we are obsessed with earning more money, we create a dream of what the future might look like. And the dream always points to comfort and self-actualization. It could be a big house on a hill, that sleek new Mercedes, or safaris in Africa. Our dreams might be less extravagant: our kids' college education, an emergency fund, or a wad of cash to donate to the church or favorite charity. Thus we try to justify our desire for the money that will realize the dream. But as we dream of a future with more money, we fail to consider what is most important. We do not consider the devotion of our hearts or God's will for our lives.

Jesus said, "No one can serve two masters, for either he will hate the one and love the other, or he will be devoted to the one and despise the other. You cannot serve God and money" (Matt. 6:24). Do you understand what Jesus is saying here? He says that loving money will make you *despise* God. Why?

Because God tells you what to do with *his* money.

Jesus is king. He owns our money. All of our blessings are from his hand, doled out from his cosmic bank of graciousness. Our money is not our money . . . and we don't like this.

Loving money displaces love for God, and it makes us forget our need for him. Because we have a measure of free will, God may allow us to have our way with money to teach us a lesson. Like Solomon, God may allow us to experience that money does not satisfy the desires of our hearts. If we are fortunate, he will crush our financial dreams and call us back to himself. If we are fortunate, he will kill our hate of him and he will end our worship of this false god. His lessons are rooted in love, and financial hardship may be just what we need to avoid making money an idol and to put God back on the throne of our lives.

The irony is that many men hate their jobs, yet this is the source of their income. If you worship money, your job should be your church, your place of worship, because it connects you to your green god. Money-hungry men want the fruit of the vine while hating the vine and not valuing their work of the vine for its own sake. They may be at their desks, in the fields, or on the job sites, but their minds are elsewhere. They want the money but not the work.

The solution to our problem is not the abandonment of money

and all material blessings. Getting rich isn't the answer, nor is becoming poor. Proverbs 30:8–9 says, "Remove far from me falsehood and lying; give me neither poverty nor riches; feed me with the food that is needful for me, lest I be full and deny you and say, 'Who is the Lord?' or lest I be poor and steal and profane the name of my God."

The solution to our money problem is an earnest, heartfelt pursuit of God. Since we cannot choose both God and money to serve, we must choose God. We must use our time, talents, and, yes, our money to pursue being near to him.

We must sell out for God.

When we sell out for God, he may bless us financially, or he may not. But we will be freed of the chains of worshiping that which does not care for us. We will be freed of our hatred of God. We will be more apt to love others and less apt to treat people as human rungs on a ladder.

You cannot serve both God and money. Which will you choose?

COMFORT

Some days it's hard to remember I live in a broken world. I wake up in an air-conditioned house underneath clean blankets next to my gorgeous wife. My kids are tucked safely asleep in their beds. I have to feel the window or check the weather on my phone to know if it's cold or hot outside before I leave for my morning run. In the summer, I walk from my cool house to the oven of my truck, which has been sitting in the sun. I blast the air conditioner, trying to escape the hardship of breaking a momentary sweat.

We think we deserve coffee. We think we deserve the right of way. We whine if our Wi-Fi goes out, and we go insane when the power goes out. Most of us have no concept of what it feels like to miss a meal or go without running water. We are accustomed to convenience.

In America, those living in poverty even have it good relative to many other people in the world. In his Forbes.com article entitled "Astonishing Numbers: America's Poor Still Live Better Than Most of the Rest of Humanity," Tim Worstall states, "The poor in the US are richer than around 70% of all the people [alive]."[2]

My point here is that we Americans—actually, those in the developed world—have it pretty good. We have food on our tables and clothes on our backs. Yet we are not satisfied. We want more food, more sleep, and more stuff.

We had better be careful, though. Comfort strangles men.

Struggle forges the heart of a man, builds his character. Be it battle, hardship, or loss, experiencing hard times heats up the steel of a man's soul so God can mold him. Forced physical hardship in the way of exercise, which we will cover in depth later in the book, creates healthy growth in the body. Likewise, forging of the spirit through hard times promotes spiritual maturity.

Comfort induces decay. It makes men soft. Comfort is the idol of idleness.

Though Jesus told us to love God with our heart and soul and mind, many of us worship comfort with our heart and soul and mind. It may be that first beer after a long day's work or the vacation you've longed for. It could be a desire for peace and quiet. We seek not the rest of the Lord but the rest of the world. We want to escape the chaos of life for a moment, so we pursue comfort in its various forms. Actually, we're hunting for numbness.

King Solomon had it all. Money, women, fame, power . . . *everything the world can offer*. Yet he provides this counsel:

> *A little sleep, a little slumber, a little folding of the hands to rest, and poverty will come upon you like a robber, and want like an armed man.*
>
> Prov. 24:33–34

Solomon got it. An idle man is a man headed for disaster. A man devoted to comfort and ease is a man who will not be satisfied. Ironically, those who obsess with comfort usually don't find it, and those who work diligently tend to enjoy a more peaceful mind.

It is easy to read the Bible like yesterday's newspaper. It is easy to treat the stories and parables like we do quotes of a famous dead person. *Good advice*, we think. I do this all too often and miss the deep riches of Holy Scripture. It is hard to relate to the ancient and foreign lifestyles of Abraham, Joseph, Isaiah, John the Baptist, and others in the Bible, given our wealthy and technologically advanced standard of living. Those guys' mode of transportation consisted of walking, or riding donkeys or camels.

Jesus and his disciples walked everywhere. Their footwear: sandals. Jesus rose early and many times stayed up all night praying. He studied voraciously as a young man and traveled endlessly during his ministry years. He went without food, sleep, and physical rest. Yet he was not a workaholic.

Jesus understood the importance of accomplishing what he was sent to accomplish. So he healed and counseled, he taught and comforted. He lived long and hard in his three decades, spreading his love and offering his rescue. He lived a *perfect* life, which was found worthy to lay down for the sins of all humankind. He knew no sin or wrongdoing. He lived rightly. He is our example.

President Theodore Roosevelt was sickly as a boy because of asthma. He could have given in and resigned himself to a life of ease. After all, he was born into a wealthy family. It would have been easy to succumb to limitations and let others do everything for him. But Roosevelt chose the opposite path, the more difficult yet beneficial way. He chose to challenge himself through sports, exercise, adventure, war, and service to others—all hardships, considering his health.

President Roosevelt explains his mind-set:

> *I wish to preach, not the doctrine of ignoble ease, but the doctrine of the strenuous life, the life of toil and effort, of labor and strife; to preach that highest form of success which comes, not to the man who desires mere easy peace, but to the man who does not shrink*

*from danger, from hardship, or from bitter toil, and
who out of these wins the splendid ultimate triumph.[3]*

Toil and effort. Labor and strife. Danger, hardship, and bitter toil. This was President Roosevelt's formula. It is a good formula for all men.

We must remove ourselves from the prison of the boring, easy life. We must strip away the veneer of comfort. It does not mean we should not enjoy life; rather, the opposite. Living a strenuous life under the mighty hand of God, spending our energy for the love of him and our neighbors, is a happy life. Some of the happiest men I know are the hardest working. The saddest? They are the worshippers of comfort.

Paul, too, was a man devoted to the strenuous life. He made tents and planted churches and traveled continually. He was jailed and beaten, yet kept on with the tasks he was responsible for. And in reading Paul's letters, I don't get the sense he was unhappy in the least. Clearly, he was happy . . . well, happy might not be the right word; rather, he was *joyful.* His purpose in sharing the gospel of Jesus Christ fueled and invigorated him.

Worshipping comfort is not the same as enjoying God's blessings. I am not decrying rest. Rest is part of God's design, and we need it. We aren't supermen. We will experience sickness and weariness that require time to be still and do nothing. But this stillness should be in stark contrast to the rest of our lives, which must be active and strenuous. So, too, we should not avoid vacations and hobbies. But, again, these activities are not to be solely a diversion from hard work. Time spent at rest and at play is meant to refresh and recharge us to continue our enjoyment of hard work.

Slaying the idol of comfort is easy in concept but hard in practice. Let me say that again: it is simple but hard. It starts with recognizing our weakness for comfort, and, as with all other idols, the battle plan to kill the hold of comfort on us is to repent of its worship and to turn our worship to Jesus.

I discovered that my pursuit of God and his ways has made me flourish, but following Jesus has also made my life more strenuous. He has called me to things I never would have done, like writing books, public speaking, business, and trying very hard—yet often failing—to live a life worthy of my calling as a man of God. A conversion to Christ is a call to action, and it will kill self-serving comfort.

Where you are lazy, become active. You are not delicate. You are a work truck, not an Italian sports car.

I have not covered all of the idols men are prone to worship. There are many others besides sex, money, and comfort, though these are common idols. We men are good at creating false gods to worship. Consider what idols you have created in your life. Have they satisfied you? Have they brought you joy? You see, you cannot put an idol in your crosshairs until you know it's there.

I can think of three reasons for the first commandment, which is "You shall have no other gods before me" (Ex. 20:3). First, no other gods exist that are real. These things we worship are not gods at all. Worshipping them is foolishness. It's like chasing the wind.

Second, God alone is worthy of all praise. He deserves it. His power and goodness reverberate throughout the world, exploding with the dawn each day. Everything beautiful and noble is of him. He has the power to create and to destroy, to judge and to redeem. He is the King.

Third, worshipping idols leads to utter disaster in our lives. It leads us astray—away from God—and arranges a future heartache of epic proportions. Let me give you an example.

When I wrote my first book, I went all in. Hearing a clear call from God to write the book, I dove in deep. I read books about writing books. I read books about how to sell books. I read books about how to build an audience. And, of course, I wrote. As I poured myself into my book, I looked for validation from others. This is where I went wrong. I mined for social media likes and feedback from my blog readers. I wanted to see if anyone noticed this epic journey I was on.

42

The validation did not come.

I began to wonder if all this work of reading, writing, and marketing was worth the time and effort. I retreated into my safe place of defensiveness, which is rather ironic—to retreat from being ignored. I wonder if anyone even noticed my crisis of not being noticed. Probably not.

Instead of putting my head down and working on my God-given call to write the book, I looked around to see if anyone was watching. I had made an idol of the approval of others. But in the months before and after the launch of the book, God helped me slay that idol. He helped me get over myself. He thickened my skin and sweetened the deal by providing encouraging feedback from readers of the book. But first I needed to kill the idol of approval. Actually, the Lord killed it for me, and I am so grateful he did. It was a bit painful, but being freed from the burden it placed on me was worth it.

If we are to become godly men of strength and character, we must become ruthlessly devoted to a war against our idols, taking no prisoners. It does not matter what we worship: as long as it is not Jesus Christ, we will whore out our hearts. We cannot be full-hearted men with our hearts removed from our bodies.

Take up your sword and slay your idols. Grant them no quarter and give them no slack. This will take serious introspection as well as a community of honest brothers who will tell you the truth. Give godly people the authority to speak truth into your life about your idols. Confess what you struggle with, and ask for their prayers. Watch God unleash himself to help you.

Once we have identified and destroyed our idols, we must move forward with reclaiming our hearts and forming our identity as men of God.

CHAPTER 4

Forming Identity

Now it happened that as he was praying alone, the disciples
were with him. And he asked them, "Who do the crowds say
that I am?" And they answered, "John the Baptist. But others
say, Elijah, and others, that one of the prophets of old has risen."
Then he said to them, "But who do you say that I am?" And Peter
answered, "The Christ of God."

—Luke 9:18–20

Now that we have established that men are very much in trouble and we've discovered the reasons why idolatry keeps us from living out faithful manhood, let us begin the work of shaping our identity.

I tried to write this book without God. In an effort to write a book that would appeal to the greatest number of men, I attempted to define manhood in such a way that a man's faith is a bolt-on to his manhood—that his faith is in addition to his manhood.

It didn't work. I couldn't do it.

In many ways it would be easier to write this book in this way; that is, without God. I could use anecdotes and opinions and shoot from the hip. I could litter the book with stories of generals and titans of industry. But by the time I wrote two chapters, I became troubled. It's not that I felt the Lord's disapproval of me, but rather that I was faking it . . . because I was. I came up with an outline that flowed well, but it wouldn't have been worth reading because I didn't believe in it. I couldn't see my way through to noble manhood without God. I couldn't even see myself in what I was writing.

I stopped writing and prayed about what I was doing, seeking God's counsel as to whether or not I should proceed with writing this godless book on manhood. The words I heard were, "Yes, but be careful."

Be careful. Those are the same words we need to heed as we think about our role as men. We must be careful that we do not try to walk a godless path in order to suit the masses.

Tremendous callings rest on the Christian man's life, things which seem impossible. The Christian man must be self-aware, humble, thoughtful, and intentional while also being a brave warrior. He must be meek in some situations and ferocious in others while, like Jesus, balancing the two. This is impossible to accomplish on our own, but with God's help it is fully doable.

Who are you? What do you stand for? You may struggle with your identity. That's okay. We all go through identity crises. Keep in mind that discovering our masculine identity is a cumulative process. It happens over time, and we often find ourselves through experiencing pain. We must be willing to let God speak into our lives. This process of letting God define us is never quick, but we must be willing to let him.

Before we move toward the ideal of noble Christian manhood, we must know who we are. Not just our names or ancestry or professions, but who we are at the core of our souls. Are we independent cocktails of DNA? Are we the kings of our destiny, or are we subjects of the King? What about our spiritual condition? Are we inherently good or bad? Once we answer these big questions, we can take our first step forward in our identity as noble Christian men.

Too many of us try to define ourselves as men solely on the basis of how we present ourselves to others. For example, the man who engages in bodybuilding in the hopes of becoming some kind of demigod is deranged—a very sad condition. No matter the size of his arms or the poundage he lifts, the mirror will never tell him what he deeply needs to know about himself. In the same way, the intellectual who defines himself by his wit will never think himself to peace. His mind is tangled because it is not linked to the Ultimate Truth. These two examples share a common characteristic: they don't start with identity; rather, they search for it through the validation of others.

Once we know who we are as human beings made in God's image, we understand who we really are. Then we are able to become the men God calls us to be, and we can work toward our identity as men.

Men are a dichotomy. We don't want anyone to tell us what to do, but at the same time we really do. I once counseled a young man who struggled with a cycle of sin and shame. I shared the gospel with him over coffee, through text messages, and by email. I told him how to pray and read his Bible. I offered practical counsel on how he might wage war on his sin. He kept asking me what he should *do*. He was tired of the same old truths of the rescue of Jesus and the power of the Spirit. Instead, he wanted me to map him out a game plan for his life—a set of actions for him to follow that would allow him to rescue himself.

That is not how the Christian life works. There is no game plan. Many people call the Bible a roadmap for life, but it isn't. The Bible is a roadmap to Jesus. We don't need a perfect strategy for living; we need to learn to live alongside our Redeemer.

Sometimes we wish God would appear, or at least send a prophet, to tell us exactly what we need to do. Maybe he could show up while we're at work, like in the story of Gideon. As Gideon was threshing his wheat, an angel showed up with a word from God. The angel told him exactly what to do (Judg. 6:12). I have longed for this kind of communication from God many times as I struggle through life. But no one can tell you what to do. It's your job as a man to discern your path by speaking to God and listening to his response. He may answer by whispering a word or sentence to you, reveal himself to you in his Word, or perhaps teach you through a friend or family member. Though I cannot tell you what to do, I can say that knowing who you are will help you know what to do.

DETHRONING YOURSELF

In Galileo's time, it was widely accepted that the sun rotated around the Earth. The Earth was the center (read: *we* were the center of the universe). This was not just a hypothesis, it was religious dogma. The Catholic Church staked a claim on this geocentric idea and included it in their set of beliefs. To disagree that the Earth was the center of the universe was heresy. Anyone teaching otherwise faced serious ramifications for upending the status quo.

The threats did not deter Galileo.

Through his research, Galileo determined through a great body of evidence that the Earth and other planets, in fact, orbit around the sun. The Earth, Galileo found, is one of many planets moving around the sun. You would think he would have been celebrated for his discovery of our heliocentric universe, but he was not. When Galileo published his findings in 1632, he was put on trial by the Inquisition in Rome and found suspect of heresy.

Walk with me into a different, but corollary, heresy. It is not a heresy against the Catholic Church, Protestant churches, or even the Bible. It is a heresy against the commonly accepted notion that you are the center of the universe and that everything orbits around you.

Stay with me for a moment, fellow heretic.

Here's the truth. You will soon rot in a grave and be largely forgotten. Your possessions will be sold or thrown away, and your money will be distributed among others. The world will go on without so much as a blink, save for the blinking tearful faces of your loved ones at your funeral. But their eyes will dry up and they, too, will soon follow you into the grave.

You are not the center of the universe. In fact, the universe does not need you.

Let's take this one step further. Not only are you not the center of your universe, but I hope to convince you that you need to remove yourself as the center of your life. It is important to understand how much you depend on God. You are the recipient of everything good in your life: your family, your money, your health, your stuff, your hobbies, *God's grace.*

It is all an ill-deserved gift.

As honored children of God, we are forgiven and grace is poured over us. The wages of sin is death, but God chooses to pay his children with love and grace instead. We cannot earn our salvation, so we don't deserve the credit. He is the center of all things, the Provider. Our role is important and we are valuable to him, but we are small in proportion to all that he is and does.

Consider how the Bible refers to The Great Prostitute in Revelation 18:7: "As she glorified herself and lived in luxury, so give her a measure of torment and mourning." She glorified herself. She put herself at the center of the universe. This is treasonous to God. Self-exaltation is what brought sin into the world in the first place. If you are at the center of your universe, dethrone yourself and remember that Jesus is King. You will be a much better man. Truly, you and I make for poor gods.

WHO DO YOU SAY HE IS?

Jesus wants us to declare who we think he is. He didn't ask his disciples what the rumors were or what other people said about him. Jesus wanted to know who *the disciples* knew Jesus to be. This question is fundamental, and how we answer this most important question will affect everything in our lives. In fact, it will cost us everything to answer it.

In *Mere Christianity*, C.S. Lewis helps frame our possible answers:

> *I am trying here to prevent anyone saying the really foolish thing that people often say about Him: I'm ready to accept Jesus as a great moral teacher, but I*

don't accept his claim to be God. That is the one thing
we must not say. A man who was merely a man and
said the sort of things Jesus said would not be a great
moral teacher. He would either be a lunatic—on the
level with the man who says he is a poached egg—or
else he would be the Devil of Hell. You must make your
choice.[1]

Who is Jesus? Our answer defines us. It directs our lives. We must make this all important declaration. If he is God, he is worthy of all praise. If he is God, we should spend our lives pursuing him. If he is not God, he's an evil liar and we should stay far away. He is either God or a sick joke. There's no in-between, which is how we often treat him: like a half god.

A man is either a follower of Jesus, or he is not. His life will tell you more than his words. The man who patterns his life after Jesus will bear fruit of the same kind as Jesus. He will be kind, loving, and brave. He will be strong, though fully dependent upon Jesus. He will serve others and spend his life so that others may live.

Too many men claim faith in Christ but live their lives without evidence of Christ's kingship. I'm not talking about being a good boy or even looking the part. That's easy. I'm not even talking about doing all the right things all the time. We can go through the motions to look like a Christian by wearing the clothing of the Christian culture and speaking the Christian lingo, but it does not make us Christians. We can read our Bibles and be nonbelievers. We can go to church and never worship.

To be a Christian means to give your whole heart away to Jesus.

A life lived with Jesus is never ordinary. It is extraordinary and scary . . . but in a good way. When Jesus calls his disciples, he doesn't ask them to get their affairs in order, pack their belongings, and meet him at the docks at 10:30. When he calls Simon Peter, James, and John—a group of partners in a fishing business—Jesus does not seem to give them much time to mull things over. *Follow me. Right now.*

Let's go. Their response? The Bible says the men "left everything and followed him" (Luke 5:11).

Meeting Jesus drastically changed the lives of the disciples, effective immediately. As they walked with Jesus, he also changed *them.* They were still imperfect men, but they now followed after a perfect Savior, and as they followed him they became more like him. They didn't change their lives to meet Jesus; they met Jesus to change their lives.

Who do you say he is?

YOUR GIVEN NAME

While other people's kids are cute, they are nothing like my own kids. Liam and Lila have my full attention. They own a part of me. I certainly care for all children, but the level of care I have for my kids is far greater than I have for any other child. I would die for my children.

I named them. They are *mine.*

We call men by all sorts of generic names: dude, man, guy, bro. These are fine, but they don't tell us anything meaningful. Our given names tell us somewhat more, as some parents give their sons a family name or one with purpose. I am pretty sure my name came from a character on a soap opera, so I'm not sure what to do with that.

We need to know what name God calls us by. It sheds a bit of light on what God thinks of us. I once counseled a guy who thought God was playing games with him. He was caught up in some dark sexual sins that he could not shake. He told me, "I think I am just supposed to live this way. I think this is the way it goes for me. I have no peace."

What does that say about his view of God? It is clear that he saw God as impotent, uninterested, or even conniving. He believed that God thought of him as a sinner, an unclean addict. No matter how I washed him with the gospel, he still felt dirty because he had not resigned his will to God, and I think he hadn't resigned his will because he believed God was not for him. He did not trust God, and he didn't know what God actually thinks of him.

Before I move on to what I believe is the most important name God gives us as men, I do not want you to make a dangerous assumption. The territory we are about to enter should unsettle you.

Do not assume that you are a Christian.

You may have grown up in church. You may be a good person. You may call on the name of Jesus as your Savior but not believe in your heart that he is *your* Savior. You may read your Bible and go to church. It is still possible that you do not know Jesus. Because you grew up in church does not mean you're a Christ follower. You cannot inherit salvation, and you can't earn it. But I have good news—the greatest news! God is not holding out on you. The door is open; Jesus made a way for you to know him, to be a true Christ follower. Before you assume you've walked through the door to eternal salvation, let's get our hands dirty.

Have you repented? Have you turned away from your sin and toward Jesus? We must be wrecked by our sins, grieved to the core. I am not asking if you're a sinless angel, for you aren't—no one is. But is your life marked by a turning from sin and a turning toward the Lord? Do you believe that Jesus is the Son of God, that he lived a perfect life, and, as a substitute for you, died on the cross as payment for your sin? Do you believe after his execution on the cross that he rose again, forever conquering sin and death? Do you trust him? Do you seek him? Most importantly, have you given your whole heart over to him, leaving nothing behind?

Here is what Jesus offers: "I am the door. If anyone enters by me, he will be saved and will go in and out and find pasture" (John 10:9).

Enter the kingdom of God by way of Jesus. He offers deep peace and comfort. He offers forgiveness and love, no matter what you've done. Trust in his perfect life, atoning death, and victorious resurrection over sin and death. Trust in his lineage, coming from the Father to earth on your behalf on a rescue mission. Lay down your attempts at earning your salvation, which the Bible likens to filthy menstrual rags. While we tried to become God, Jesus came to earth to become one of us. He is Immanuel, which means "God with us."

If we enter by the door of Jesus, the Lord gives us a *new name*. "But to all who did receive him, who believed in his name, he gave the right to become children of God, who were born not of blood nor of the will of the flesh nor of the will of man, but of God" (John 1:12–13).

Do you see it? Can you believe it? Here is the name we are given: if we receive Jesus and believe in him, we are children of God. We are his *sons*.

This changes everything.

If we are in Christ, we are born of God. New hearts, new lenses, and, yes, new *manhood*.

This is why I could not write a book about manhood without God. It is impossible for me, because my manhood is wrapped up in my identity as a true son of God. Everything proceeds from that basis, even to the core of my soul.

Consider the implications of our sonship:

- If we are God's sons, he protects us.
- If we are God's sons, he is for us.
- If we are God's sons, we are heirs of the King.
- If we are God's sons, we are from the kingdom of heaven.

Knowing this, your first move is to turn from an outward definition of your manhood, from what others think of you, how you look, how you act, or what has been said about you. What matters is what God says about you, and what he says about you is that you are his *son*. You have access to the throne because of the work of Jesus on the cross. If you trust in Christ, you are a son of the royal family.

My dad is my hero. He is an outstanding man who was my first example of manhood, and he is still the best example I know. I am thirty-three, but I am still learning from him, and I always will. We should assume the same posture with God as his sons. We should learn from him, listen to him, and emulate him—forever.

My dad and I have always enjoyed spending time together. We can be in a business meeting (yes, we are in business together) or chasing English Pointers on a quail hunt, it does not matter. We enjoy the presence of each other. Likewise, we should enjoy our time with God, which happens to be every moment of every day. He is omnipresent, so we should never forget to enjoy our time with him. Acknowledge him when the wind changes and you get the scent of a rosebush. He is playfully wooing you. *He is here.*

Sometimes God is less than playful, though. I remember sitting on a porch with a group of men at a beautiful Texas ranch as a thunderstorm approached. The flashes of lightning drew near, but we didn't move. The cool air on the front of the storm was pleasant and it wasn't raining yet, so we just hung tight. We enjoyed watching the storm approach. Until . . .

Crack! BOOM!

Lightning struck a tree dangerously close to us. It was so near it rattled our chests. We were on our feet before we knew what had happened.

Sometimes God calls through the scent of roses on the breeze, and other times he explodes an oak tree right next to you. But he is never silent. He is after you. When we recognize this and, in turn, pursue him, our joy will multiply and deepen. Our manhood will flourish, and we will solidify our identity.

I want to end with a prayer. Find somewhere quiet, away from all distractions. Do it now. Pray with me:

Father, I trust you. I believe I am saved by the blood of Jesus, by his work for me on the cross. In loving anguish he delivered my soul. God, make me a man. Make me your man. I do not want to be my own man; I want to be your son. Father me. Teach me. Guide me. Direct me on the path to my true identity so that on the way I might find more of you. In the holy name of Jesus, amen.

CHAPTER 5

Show Yourself a Man

When David's time to die drew near, he commanded Solomon his son, saying, "I am about to go the way of all the earth. **Be strong, and show yourself a man,** *and keep the charge of the Lord your God, walking in his ways and keeping his statutes, his commandments, his rules, and his testimonies, as it is written in the Law of Moses, that you may prosper in all that you do and wherever you turn, that the Lord may establish his word that he spoke concerning me, saying, 'If your sons pay close attention to their way, to walk before me in faithfulness with all their heart and with all their soul, you shall not lack a man on the throne of Israel.'"*

—1 Kings 2:1–4 (emphasis mine)

King David is dying. The man who slayed Goliath and reigned over Israel for forty years lies in his palace, shivering. He cannot get warm. The man whom God called "a man after my heart" gasps for breath. His eyes are bloodshot; his skin thin and gray.

David fought many battles. He expanded the kingdom of Israel. He made many mistakes, but his life is, well, larger than life. As he lies on his death bed, the kingdom waits, holding its breath. As he lay dying, his son Adonijah claims the crown. He uses the presumptive close, a sales tactic that assumes the prospective buyer has agreed to the purchase. He gathers men and assumes the posture of the nation's king. But Adonijah is not to be king. David promised the throne to one of his other sons. He promised Bathsheba that their son Solomon would be king.

Thus, Solomon is anointed king. He takes the throne, just as his father decreed. Adonijah trembles, fearing for his life because he had seriously stepped on Solomon's toes. Solomon probably trembles too, but for different reasons.

Solomon is now king. His legendary father is dying. No longer just an honored member of the king's family, Solomon now stands on his own two feet as Israel's sovereign—a weighty responsibility. David's are massive shoes to fill.

Imagine the scene as David summons Solomon to his chamber. Expensive blankets cover David. Because he could not get warm, his servants found the most beautiful woman in the kingdom to lie in his arms to generate body heat. Trays of food and various drinks surround the large bed. David's attendants jump at any opportunity to make him more comfortable.

Solomon walks in. His hands are moist with sweat, and his stomach churns. He already mourns his father, and he understands the purpose of this meeting: his father's legacy, the kingdom of Israel. He knows that his father will give him a charge and a blessing, and though he'd rather the circumstances be different, Solomon is anxious to hear his father's words.

He goes to his father's side.

David turns his head, looking deep into Solomon's eyes. He musters his weak breath, and with the energy he has left he speaks. "I am about to go the way of all the earth. *Be strong, and show yourself a man . . .*"

Be a *man*, Solomon.

Square your shoulders and be *brave*, Solomon.

Be *strong*, Solomon.

Embrace your God-given *authority*, Solomon.

BE A MAN.

SHOW YOURSELF A MAN

The majority of the translators of this Hebrew text agree that David's command to Solomon is gendered. That is, he was not telling Solomon to merely be a man in the universal sense, as in "be a human." Rather, David tells Solomon to be who God made him to be. A man. It is apparent that David meant for Solomon to be utterly masculine in his kingship, to be strong and brave and faithful.

We find similar versions of David's charge elsewhere in the Bible. After Moses dies, Joshua steps into the leadership role. The Lord commands him to "be strong and courageous." He commands Joshua not to fear, for the Lord is with him everywhere he goes.

When the Philistines heard Israel shouting in victory after capturing the Ark of the Covenant, they trembled. The Philistines knew the power of Israel's God. They were terrified of Israel because of the backing of their mighty God. As the Philistines huddle amidst the victory roar of Israel, they charged each other to "be men and fight."

When David commands Solomon to build the temple, he tells him to "be strong and courageous and do it." He then prays over Solomon: "Grant to Solomon my son a whole heart that he may keep your commandments, your testimonies, and your statutes" (1 Chron. 29:19).

Courage and strength and faithfulness are not exclusively masculine traits, of course. But they are at the heart of what a man should be. He should be strong and capable. He should be brave enough to step into the battles of life *like a man*. He should be faithful to God and his words as they are revealed in Scripture.

Though he is hard to describe, you know this kind of man when you encounter him. You know when you're in the presence of a godly man. He is at once interesting and a little intimidating, though he is usually humbly unaware. He is merely himself. When you leave his presence, you are changed. That is because you've been changed by his love, or rather the love he's received by Christ, which flows through him to all he meets. It gets on you. You catch it like a cold.

This is markedly different from the stereotypical manly man who puts on the tough-guy act. He may intimidate, but he does not exude the power of love. The common theme in these preceding verses is that being a man means being faithful to God. It means praying to him, listening to him, and reading the treasure trove of Scripture. These actions are, in the words of David, the sign of a man having a *whole heart*. A man with a whole heart—that is, a heart fully given to the Lord—can be strong and courageous because of God's work in him.

But to what end does he devote his strength and bravery? This matters a great deal. Faithfulness to the noble purpose of God makes all the difference. It is what makes a man a godly man.

CALLING THE WEAKLINGS

Have you ever thought about who in your life you'd like to have next to you in battle? Who would you put next to you when the bullets start flying? Maybe I'm weird, but I have considered it. I'd want someone brave, trustworthy, and strong. I'd want someone who is not obsessed with self-preservation and who cares about others enough to die for them. That's how I'd choose. I know men like this, and they are my brothers in the trenches of life's battles.

Consider the men God taps to do his work. He doesn't choose the biggest, strongest, or even bravest. He doesn't choose the super-heroes or the geniuses. He does not even choose the highest quality of men. He surprises us. Consider Paul, the persecutor. Or David, the man who kills the husband of his extra-marital fling. Or Peter, who denies Jesus not once but three times. God does not pick the best men.

He builds them.

Let's get back to Gideon. Israel was under the oppressive hands of Midian. As soon as the Israelites' crops were ready for reaping, their enemies swooped in and stole the harvest, laying the land bare—like a bully taking the puny kid's lunch. This demoralized Israel.

Israel cried out to God, so he sent a prophet to the people of Israel, assuring them that God had heard their cries and had a plan to rescue them. His plan relied upon a runt.

Gideon, a very average man, came from the weakest of the clans in the area; he's a runt among runts. Our story picks up as he is in the field threshing wheat in a winepress. As he works, he hides from the Midianites so they won't steal his harvest like they always do.

As Gideon hurries to finish his task, an angel appears out of nowhere and sits under a tree near Gideon. "The Lord is with you, O mighty man of valor" (Judg. 6:12).

You have to imagine Gideon jumping out of his skin. He is weak. He is scared. He is hiding. He is not a mighty man of valor, and he knows it. But the angel is not being sarcastic, nor is the angel ignorant of who Gideon is. The angel arrives with a word from the Lord and greets Gideon exactly as he should. It takes a moment for us to understand why as the story continues.

Gideon backpedals. He questions himself and his clan. In doing so, he questions God. But God does not back down. God is after Gideon. He has a mission for him. The angel explains what Gideon is to do, and though Gideon is woefully underequipped for the mission he's given, he obeys. That's what helps him become a mighty man of valor: not his strength but his obedience. God will do the work for him if he'll just say yes.

Gideon goes on to defeat the Midianites, but not before God further stacks the odds against Israel. God does not want Israel to think they've defeated the Midianites on their own, so he gives them a runt leader from the runt clan, and then he reduces their forces to 300 men. When Midian retreats, it is clearly not because of the strength of the Israelites. It is their God.

Notice how when God calls ordinary men to extraordinary things, he brings great glory upon himself, and he brings great honor upon the man he calls. His glory is the goal, but the bonus is that the man who says yes tends to receive honor and walks away from the completed task forever changed.

David learned this as well. As a young man he defeated Goliath on the battlefield when no one would man up and face the giant Philistine. David understood that God uses underdogs. He said yes and God made a man of him. Imperfect men highlight God's perfection. Weak men highlight his strength. And it sure is fun when his power moves through you.

Showing yourself a man is not about chest-beating bravado. Rather, it is humility combined with the strength of God. It is courage in the face of fear because God is bigger. God does not call the superheroes; he calls the runts like you and me and Gideon.

If you think God has called you to something you are ill-equipped for, pay attention. If he has made you want to do something that makes you tremble, *good*. You are in good company. Remember, Jesus sweat blood in anguish over his duty to die a cruel death on a cross. God will call you to what you cannot do to show you what *he* can do. When you answer that call, that's *showing yourself a man*.

WALKING IN HIS WAYS

Though I know how God calls me to live, I sometimes choose to chart my own course. I create idols and devote myself to them. My obsessions over things like fly fishing, jiu-jitsu, lifting weights, writing, or any number of things shows the posture of my heart. My mind goes to my obsessions during quiet times, and I hate this. I get on obsessive kicks and focus intensely on something for a period of time until I tire of it. This isn't just a personality flaw; it shows I am promiscuous with my worship. Thankfully, God in his mercy shoots my idols through the face with arrows: "For you will not put them to flight; you will aim at their faces with your bows" (Ps. 21:12).

David tells Solomon to walk in God's ways, to follow the ancient path of wisdom and truth. Maybe he knows Solomon is prone to walk in his own ways, like me. David was no stranger to the wayward path, so he knew what to look for.

Walking in the ways of God is primarily about two things: trust and walking in the Spirit.

First, let's look more closely at trust. To walk in God's ways requires trust. We must trust that what God says is true and that he is never, ever holding out on us. This may sound easy, but it isn't. Not at all. To trust God means to submit our lives to him, and that includes *everything*. We pack up our money, our dreams, our families, and our time and drag it home to God. What will he do with it?

He is not like a tow truck driver. He won't take your stuff to his lot and demand you pay to get it back. Jesus tells us in Luke 11:11–13, "What father among you, if his son asks for a fish, will instead of a fish give him a serpent; or if he asks for an egg, will give him a scorpion? If you then, who are evil, know how to give good gifts to your children, how much more will the heavenly Father give the Holy Spirit to those who ask him!"

Wanting a happy life is not unreasonable. It is not sinful. Of course we want to be happy. So when we, through various words and prayers, try to tell God that we want to be happy, he gets it. When we submit our lives to walk in his ways, he will not give us scorpions and snakes in return. He will give us only what is good for us: "Every good gift and every perfect gift is from above, coming down from the Father of lights, with whom there is no variation or shadow due to change" (James 1:17).

This is so simple. God made the earth and everything in it by the power of his voice. He knows how everything works because he made everything. As I write these words using my keyboard, I do so with dexterity and clarity because God made my brain synapses fire in just the right way. We have this little thing in our hearts called the sinoatrial node. It is like a natural pacemaker that shocks our hearts to life. It enables us to live for decades disconnected from a visible power source. Our subservience to God's design is obvious, yet we don't notice it. It's like scrambling for your car keys when they are already in your hand.

If God designed us and the world in which we inhabit, it should naturally follow that we can trust him to tell us how to flourish. How should we live in this place he made for us? Because his every word is true, we can trust that all of his commands are designed to help us on our way through this world and into the next. That's why David told Solomon to walk in God's ways; he knew it'd be best for Solomon.

Second, walking in his ways means walking in the Spirit. I know this sounds ethereal. It is. It's hard to explain. But it's very important to understand.

When Jesus ascended into heaven, the Spirit moved into the bodies of his followers. It's not that the Spirit just hovers around everywhere like a smoky genie. He lives within the hearts of believers; he indwells them. God is in us.

Walking in God's ways is not a maze. He has us by the hand. To paraphrase the band Needtobreathe, there is a crack in the door of our lives with blinding light behind it.[1] It is the door to a life in tune with the Spirit of God. Through prayer and awareness, we need to yank that door open to intimacy with the Spirit.

When we read the Bible, the Spirit massages the truths of Scripture into our hearts. You may think you're reading Matthew for the sixth time, but the Spirit knows you need to see in a new way how Jesus handles a certain parable. The Spirit will pluck the words perfectly and deposit them into your soul. Perhaps you don't understand the Bible and you think it's for varsity Christians and preachers. It isn't. It is for us all. And I promise if you'll read it, God will meet you there.

Prayer is an embrace, not a presentation. It should not be awkward and hard. We have made prayer a performance, which is why many people will not pray aloud in front of others. The assumption is that some people are good at praying and others aren't. That's like saying some people are good at breathing while others aren't. Prayer is fundamental to spiritual life.

It's okay to pray quietly and in secret. Jesus endorsed that. Some people are introverts so corporate prayer will be uncomfortable. But I urge the introverts among us to push through the fear and into a humble conversation with God, regardless of whether you're praying alone or with fellow believers. Prayer is talking to our daddy, not reciting poetry to English professors.

David wanted Solomon to walk in the ways of God. Nothing will impact you more than walking in God's ways and submitting yourself to his fatherhood. A godly father has no greater hope than to see his children walk in God's ways with a whole heart. God will father you and make you a man. "Who is the man who fears the Lord? Him will he instruct in the way that he should choose" (Ps. 25:12).

PAYING CLOSE ATTENTION TO YOUR WAY

To journey ever toward God, no matter the difficulty and pain experienced along the way, is rewarding. One of the most remarkable results of the journey is increased intimacy with God. Although this precious connection is more than enough, God further blesses us.

The hope of Christ offers the believer great joy. In contrast to this joy, we should be disgusted with our sin. We should not tolerate anything that separates us from Jesus. Please don't confuse disgust or intolerance with self-deprecation, masochism, or asceticism. We do not grow closer to God by abusing ourselves. What I mean is this: the longer you walk with God, the more aware you will be of your sins. Sometimes it feels like a cycle of madness to shed sinful behaviors and attitudes yet grow in awareness of your brokenness. But this awareness is good, as it causes us to initiate the desired cycle of repentance and trust. Sin . . . repentance . . . forgiveness . . . trust. Repeat.

The irony here is that as we grow in awareness of our depravity, we are sanctified and become more like Jesus. We do become better men over time. But if with our betterment, pride grows with our own righteousness, we are spiritually ill. We should grow in grace and holiness as well as grow in awareness of our shortcomings. This is not to diminish the man; it is to broadcast the glory of God. And glorifying God sweetens a man's soul and makes him happy and joyful.

The man covered in vomit who lays among empty bottles and wakes up in an alley knows he is a mess. If he meets Jesus, he will meet the man of grace. Jesus will pick him up and hold him in his arms; then the man's life will begin to change, for he begins an inward change. As our man grows in sanctification, he will perhaps be delivered from his abusive drinking. But that does not mean he's holy; it just means he is sober. Other dark spots in his heart bring forth various sins: pride, anger, lust, and more. His life will be much nearer to being Christ-like, but he still has much work to do—and he will probably sense it. God still has much work to do in the man. This inward change is a long game. The bitter truth is that we never stop growing in our need for grace. Thank God we don't. Our brokenness, no matter how blatant or hidden, brings us to our knees before the throne of grace.

So is sin a good thing? Of course not. But what we mean for evil, God will use for good. He will pick us up, discipline us, embrace us, and send us on our way on his path. This keeps us humble and reliant upon God, which is a healthy posture for a man.

As time goes on in our walk with Jesus, we need to pay increasingly closer attention to ourselves. Even if some of our big sins are killed, others lurk beneath the surface. They are alive and well in our hearts. The sins we hide are dangerous. They will kill a man. But the sins we are unaware of are the worst, which is why we must pay close attention to ourselves.

A THREEFOLD CORD

Ecclesiastes 4:10–12 tells us,

> *For if they fall, one will lift up his fellow. But woe to him who is alone when he falls and has not another to lift him up! Again, if two lie together, they keep warm, but how can one keep warm alone? And though a man might prevail against one who is alone, two will withstand him—a threefold cord is not quickly broken.*

Guess who wrote this verse? Solomon. Whether God taught him this lesson through experience or through his father, Solomon clearly picked up on this vital component of walking in God's ways. To be strong and show yourself a man, you need to surround yourself with good men.

This is easy for extroverts. They seem to absorb energy from being around people. But this is much harder for introverts, who get their energy from being alone or in small groups. As a general rule, extroverts need to listen more and introverts need to talk more. And they both need to be in a strong community with other believing men.

Building a fellowship with other men could look many different ways, and, frankly, none of them are convenient. We must fight for our brotherhood. It could be church-sanctioned or organic. It could be a discipleship group or just a group of friends. It could be two men or it could be ten. Of course, a discipleship group is more intense and focused. In these groups, I believe it is crucial when meeting to rally around Scripture. But no matter the group dynamic, men need other men.

You may wonder why it is so important for men to be around men. First, we need to have fun with other men. We will get into the topic of adventure and building the heart in chapter eight, but suffice it to say that having a good time with other men tests us, builds us, and ministers to us.

Second, we need to be held accountable by other men. We need to have thick skin in our friendships so our brothers can call us on our sins and stupidity. If I see you drowning but keep my mouth shut because I don't want to embarrass you, I clearly don't care about you. We must speak up when a brother is heading down a dangerous path.

Third, we need the shared strength of our brothers. Human beings are tribal by nature. God made us this way. A threefold cord is not easily broken because of the combined strength of its members. So too, when we stand with our brothers, we stand in strength. With shared faith and energy, we can accomplish much. With isolation, we wither.

YOUR CHARGE

David tells Solomon to be strong and show himself a man. He calls Solomon to a high standard of manly living, one in sync with God. I can imagine the intensity with which the dying David spoke these words to his son. I can picture the glint in his eye. I bet he mustered whatever strength remained in his feeble body and branded the words onto Solomon's heart. His father's words must have helped Solomon become a man. And the charge is as relevant to us today as it was for Solomon.

This is not a halftime speech. It is not a motivational poster. It is a tattoo on your heart. Mandatory. Irrevocable.

Where have you fallen short as a man? Is it your courage? Then take courage, my brother. The Lord goes with you. Move toward your fears. Stand toe-to-toe with them as a son of God. The army of heaven stands with you.

Is it holiness? Then take up your sword and slay your sins. But don't do it alone. Ask Jesus for his help and then ask a brother to join you in your battle.

It does not matter where or how you have fallen short. The answer is the same: Jesus. His forgiveness. His grace. His power. His mercy. His strength.

If you have never been given a charge like this, take a moment to drink it in. God is intentional in his love for us, and it is no accident that you are reading these words. If you are a man, God calls you to step forward into faithful, manly living under his Kingship.

He calls you to be strong and show yourself a man.

CHAPTER 6

Open Your Mind

But the wisdom from above is first pure, then peaceable, gentle, open to reason, full of mercy and good fruits.

—James 3:17

"I'm not a reader."
I hear men say this all the time, and it takes the wind out of me. Really? You aren't a reader? Though some have valid reading disorders—e.g., dysgraphia, dyslexia, and the like—reading is not an innate talent. It is a choice, one that, as men, we must make if we want to be men of godly virtue. Part of showing yourself a man is to grow your mind. If you aren't a reader, I hope to convince you to become one.

Effective men are curious learners. They realize their limit of knowledge and want to know more. They humbly seek wisdom while gaining knowledge. Theodore Roosevelt was a voracious reader, sometimes speed-reading up to three books per day. Winston Churchill made reading a priority in his schedule, as did Benjamin Franklin. Nearly all of the great men throughout history were avid readers. We must expand our perspectives beyond our personal experiences, and books help us do this.

The problem is that many of us have grown complacent with our knowledge. Maybe we went to college and believe we're educated. Further, with the kind and amount of technology at our fingertips, we can instantly find the information we need . . . just ask Siri. Google search results—millions—are just seconds away. We have grown intellectually lazy. Not only that, our readily available technology has rewired our brains so that it is it difficult for us to focus our attention. A man overly reliant on technology is an underdeveloped man because his mind is not challenged to grow.

A grave danger of the "I'm not a reader" mentality is that it leads men to avoid reading Scripture altogether, for the man who does not read tends to avoid the pages of Scripture. This is ignoring the treasure of God.

Our modern age has changed our brains so that it has become harder to nourish our minds. It seems many of us believe long-form study and deep thought are unnecessary, even irrelevant. Nothing is wrong with quick access to information, but the problem asserts itself when we become dependent upon technology and let it do the thinking for us. What's worse is we create opinions based on random articles and blogs, which tend to be binary (holding one extreme view or the other). We take someone else's opinion and make it our own instead of formulating our own view based on evidence or critical thinking.

You may think that with that last paragraph I have contradicted myself. First I said to read, then I was critical of reading blogs and Internet articles. Please don't miss my point. Casual reading has its place, but it should not replace books of substance that challenge us to become better, wiser, more informed godly men.

I have picked up and put down *The Brothers Karamazov* by Fyodor Dostoyevsky several times. It is a long and hard book, and I have struggled to get traction. I pick it up, get distracted, and it ends up back on the shelf. I am bound and determined to read it. If I never read it, I will miss this kind of treasure: "The awful thing is that beauty is mysterious as well as terrible. God and the devil are fighting there and the battlefield is the heart of man."[1]

That's good stuff, isn't it? If we allow ourselves to remain distracted and never dive into great books like *The Brothers Karamazov*, we will miss out on the abundant beauty and wisdom within the pages of great books. They will not read themselves. We must crack them open.

With the advent of social media, email, and instant information, our attention spans have shortened to adapt to this new environment. We jump from feed to feed, email account to email account, scanning for relevant data. Notifications ping our attention away from our work or being present with our families. This frenzy forces us to remain on the surface, but the riches are down deep. We are broad but not deep. When we go deep in thought—or, even better, in prayer—we make use of the powerful brain God has given us (and we connect with the source of all wisdom and knowledge). We put it through the paces of exercise. This is good for us.

Reading books helps to rewire the brain for attentive thought. I think physical books are the best, as they do not allow us to click or surf our way away from our train of thought. A study in Norway found increased reading retention for readers of paper books versus e-readers (like a Kindle, iPad, or Nook). Amy Craft, the leading researcher of this study, believes this increase in retention might be owed to the fact that when reading a physical book, your fingers can sense the progress of turning pages. Your fingers carry you through the story as you turn pages.[2] Also, there is something special about a paper book in the hands. Paper books have a wonderful smell that becomes Pavlovian as you learn to enjoy reading. Whether fiction or nonfiction, a book can transport you into another world. Want to travel in time? Read a book. They are portals.

In a *Harvard Business Review* article titled "For Those Who Want to Lead, Read," John Coleman frames the issue:

> *Even as global literacy rates are high (84%), people are reading less and less deeply. The National Endowment for the Arts (PDF) has found that "[r]eading has declined among every group of adult Americans,"*

*and for the first time in American history, "less than
half of the U.S. adult American population is reading
literature." Literacy has been improving in countries
like India and China, but that literacy may not
translate into more or deeper reading.[3]*

We can read, but we don't—at least not deeply. There's even a
word for this problem: aliteracy. *Merriam-Webster* defines aliteracy as
"the quality or state of being able to read but uninterested in doing so."
Most of us can read, but many of us are aliterate.

Growing the mind is not just for scholars. All men would be
better men if their minds were sharpened and massaged with knowledge. God has called men to be leaders, and a leader with a well-read
mind will communicate better, have a better context with which to
make decisions, and will be astute in the study of human behavior.
Of course, the opposite is true as well. The leader who does not read
has stunted communication skills, has less context to use in decision making, and is less informed of human nature. He will probably
make decisions based on emotion rather than intellect, which is a
recipe for disaster.

It does not matter your profession or your social standing. It
does not matter if you have a college degree or an eighth-grade education. A man who chooses to educate himself will never regret it,
for knowledge is indeed power. Education—whether self-directed
or through formal schooling—grants a man the power of perspective
and wisdom. It helps him think clearly, which will aid him in living
a meaningful life.

It is easy to confuse intellect with education. If someone possesses college degrees, we might think of him as smart, but he may or
may not be. He has just shown he has the requisite intelligence to get
through higher education, which many people do. My point is that
you aren't smart because you went to college, and you aren't dumb
if you didn't. We must move away from wondering whether we are
"smart" and instead focus on learning and seeking wisdom.

Also, it is easy to confuse education with knowledge. We may wrongly assume a college graduate is knowledgeable. After all, his diploma proves it. But a truly learned man has devoted himself to the pursuit of knowledge. That is available to all of us.

The Bible warns us that knowledge puffs up (1 Cor. 8:1). It is easy to become bloated with information, which can make us prideful. But our pride is not well-founded. The more we learn, the more we learn how much we *don't know*. (In this way it is a lot like the sanctification process: the more you grow, the more you know you need to grow.) Learning is training in humility. Of course, chances are that a well-read man will know far more facts or particulars about an event, era, or historical figure than the man who never reads or pursues knowledge. An English major may know the precise word to use in a sentence, whereas the ignorant man is clueless. The man with a well-developed mind certainly has an advantage. We see a contrast that exists between an educated man, including a self-educated man, and an uneducated one.

Abraham Lincoln famously said, "Better to remain silent and be thought a fool than to speak out and remove all doubt." I have thought about this quote many times in my life, and it has helped me avoid speaking before thinking. It is an excellent mind-set. If I may create a variation of Lincoln's words, I believe it is also *better to remain silent and be thought average than to speak out to try to prove you are wise*. No one needs to know how many books you've read or where you went to school. Like the trained martial artist who remains silent about his capability to fight, wisdom is a secret we should hold close, only to be used in the proper moments. It is not a badge we wear in hopes of cultivating a better reputation. The cultivation of a *humble mind* (1 Peter 3:8) is the godly path.

As with the body, some men are blessed naturally with a strong mind. Some handle numbers with ease, while others write or remember history. We are all endowed with different mental gifts, and to different degrees. Mental illnesses and learning disabilities make learning difficult for some. Here again the call is not to perfection but to *stewardship*—to caring for what we've been given. The mind is a gift from God. It is to be sharpened and used, not to be neglected or overly inflated. It is the best tool a man has by far, for the mind can guide and direct the body. Although our bodies and minds will fail as we age and face life in a broken world, no one can take the wisdom of our minds. The mind cannot be repossessed or foreclosed upon.

THE CURIOUS MIND OF JESUS

Jesus was curious. As he grew up, he studied and learned passionately. When he was twelve, his parents took him to Jerusalem for the Feast of the Passover, as was the custom for Jews. Though at this point in his life he was just a boy attending the event with his family, Jesus would later become the ultimate Passover, his blood marking our forgiveness and purchasing us freedom from God's wrath.

After the feast was over, Jesus's parents left Jerusalem and headed home. They thought Jesus was somewhere in their travel group. It wasn't until the end of the day that they could not find him anywhere, and they freaked out. They searched for days to find Jesus, backtracking to Jerusalem. If you've ever lost track of a child for even five minutes, you've tasted the terror Joseph and Mary must have felt.

Here is how they found him: "After three days they found him in the temple, sitting among the teachers, listening to them and asking them questions. And all who heard him were amazed at his understanding and his answers" (Luke 2:46–47).

Jesus was enthralled by the teaching in the temple. So captivated, he wanted to learn all about it; thus, he stayed behind when his parents went home. *Better to ask for forgiveness than permission*, he might have thought. Jesus was carried away by what he was hearing, about wisdom so deep it transforms eternities. It touched his soul, resonating deeply within. This was the foundation of his ministry: a humble and curious mind. He searched and reasoned and questioned. We would be wise men to emulate this young Jesus. We would be wise to seek his wisdom.

I have a bird dog named Titus. He is young and has not hunted yet, but his instincts are powerful. When we go for a run, his eyes scan for prey. His nose sniffs for a sign. If I let him off leash and do not recall him, it is easy for him to get carried away on a scent trail left by an animal. He can get lost. It's not that he intends to wander off; it's that he is so immersed in the chase. So it was with Jesus and the temple. He was so focused on learning that he got carried away. So it should be with each of us.

FRAMING THE WORLD

C. S. Lewis famously wrote, "I believe in Christianity as I believe that the Sun has risen, not only because I see it, but because by it I see everything else."[4]

This quote, the last line in Lewis's paper "Is Theology Poetry?" written for the Oxford Socratic Club, is given as the punch line of Lewis's argument that the Christian faith provides a basis or starting point for science and the arts. Lewis argues that science without God is nihilism—that is, nothing.

> *If minds are wholly dependent on brains, and brains on bio-chemistry, and bio-chemistry (in the long run) on the meaningless flux of the atoms, I cannot understand how the thought of those minds should have any more significance than the sound of the wind in the trees.*[5]

The faithless man can gather knowledge, but he does not have anywhere to put it, at least not anywhere that has meaning. Knowledge without God is unframed, like a masterpiece painted on gravel. Faith affords a coherent framework. If, for example, I learn about the chemical reaction in the brain when one experiences what we call "love," I can relate this knowledge to God's design and marvel at his brilliance. It gives love a deeper meaning. If I do not have that faith for a rational basis point, this knowledge must be attributed to something more carnal, like herd mentality or evolution. It becomes a meaningless, random chemical reaction. If you have loved or been loved, you know it is much deeper than herd mentality or incidental impulses of the brain. If you have loved a woman, you understand your love was rooted in a realm outside of this world. The love of a woman is not just about physically knowing her; it's about knowing her soul. Framing the science of love within God's design makes sense.

Faith is much more than a cosmic filing cabinet for education, of course. One must not believe so he can make sense of the world; he can make sense of the world because he believes.

We do not exist in a pool of a meaningless flux of atoms. We live in the kingdom of the Creator. He is here with us, growing flowers and firing brain synapses. Within the frame of faith, each moment of learning—or, for that matter, every moment of every day—becomes part of a great story. God weaves everyday moments together on the canvas of history to tell his epic story of redemption. Our faith helps us hear his voice in what we see, read, and hear.

TAKE THE TIME

In a world of clickbait and quick fixes, it seems boring or prudish to devote yourself to old-fashioned ways of learning—physical books, research, critical thinking, etc. It makes you a weirdo at best or a nerd at worst. *No one needs to sit around and do this stuff anymore.*

I get it. It's hard to sit down and read a book while the television emits its siren song. Your phone, holding worlds of knowledge, teases you with flickering entertainment. That old book seems like the last thing you'd choose. Focus is hard. But focused reading grows the mind and encourages deep thought. We are not built for imminent distraction, though that is where we find ourselves too often. A book, or any form of focused study, engages the brain to think until it's tired from thinking. It is like going for a long run with your thoughts.

What distracting entertainment (social media, television, web surfing) offers is exhaustion from having a million options at once. It is overload of the wrong kind that leaves you wrung out and no smarter or happier. It's a bag full of candy.

With all the digital media in our lives, it can feel like we're drowning, which the band Thrice laments in their song "Digital Sea." The chorus begins with the line "I am drowning in a digital sea."[5] I think many of us can relate.

Growing our minds makes us sharper men, and it equips us for good living. It is not an end in and of itself. It is preparation to live a rich life, and the process of learning should be a joyful experience. As men, when we expand our minds, we give ourselves more tools to use, more capability. We become better tools in God's hands. The more we know, the more clearly we see. God's glory is magnified.

We need another quote from Abraham Lincoln: "Give me six hours to chop down a tree and I will spend the first four sharpening the axe." To some, this may seem like a ridiculous waste of time; that is, until you try to cut down a tree with a dull axe. Lincoln was correct to sharpen his axe first; thereby making his task easier. Learning is sharpening the axe of our minds. It makes us better able to deal with our constantly changing lives.

This takes time, of course. It seems counterintuitive to devote time to learning. Even reading a great novel can seem like time wasted in our hurried culture, but literature makes us thoughtful men, ready to approach the forest of life.

Hear what Billy Graham has to say about this in a 2011 interview with *Christianity Today*:

> Interviewer: If you could, would you go back and do anything differently?
>
> Graham: Yes, of course. I'd spend more time at home with my family, and I'd study more and preach less.[6]

Throughout his ministry, Mr. Graham was the vehicle through which countless people met the risen Jesus. He was effective in his ministry. But Mr. Graham understood that he could have preached more efficiently with a sharper axe: fewer but better sermons.

This is the dragon I fight in my writing. It is easy for me to slap words onto a page. I do not stare at a blinking cursor and wonder what I'll write next, as some do. But it doesn't mean what I write will be any good. It is only through prayer, study, and engaged thought that I write anything worth reading. I find that God meets me at the keyboard when I spend time sharpening my axe. Dragging a dull axe to the keyboard results in my regurgitating my own thoughts, opinions, and experiences. Not interesting and not helpful. I am a better writer and more effective communicator when I bring my axe sharpened through prayer, study, research, and reading.

MASSAGING THE HEART

Ultimately, knowledge is not about filling your head with facts. It is not about a resume of books read or classes taken or a vocabulary stuffed with big words. These are externally focused, mere symptoms of learning. We do well to focus on the internal—that is, the heart. Growing the mind is ultimately about sowing seeds in the heart.

We should be after a deeper union with God. He is after a deeper union with us. As we explore him and interact with the truth—territory owned and established by him—we will learn more about him, and, thus, it should naturally follow that we worship him more. This should be an ever present cycle in our lives.

When I was in college, I had a spiritual awakening. I had realized, by trial and copious error, that I could find no joy in the bottom of a whiskey bottle. By God's grace, he used Lindsay, whom I was dating at the time, as a tender instrument to sanctify me and draw me closer to him. I was on a path toward deeper union with him. But he was about to take me deeper.

Lindsay's parents had invited me to join the family on a vacation to Gulf Shores, Alabama, a quiet coastal town whose beaches boast white sand and gentle waves. We settled into a rented condo with a central common area and a sliding glass door overlooking the light blue waters. We cracked the sliding glass door and the salty air filled the condo.

During a quiet time of the day, I settled into my room with C. S. Lewis's *Mere Christianity*. The reading challenged me, for Lewis wrote in a different time and place, and his brilliant arguments were sometimes hard to follow. I knew what he was saying was true as I read it, but it took me some time to understand it. His logic was spring-loaded; as you read it the spring tightened and tightened until finally Lewis made his point. When Lewis's arguments sprang, it struck like a jolt of energy to my soul. I had never interacted with a book like this before. It carried me away. I could not put it down.

Lewis set out to disprove Christianity but ended up proving to himself that it is true. As the book went on, Lewis knocked down many of my intellectual objections to Christianity—some of which I didn't know I held until I faced them through his writing. He also built up fortresses of reason around the truth of Christianity, strengthening my faith.

Mere Christianity is not Scripture, of course. But I do believe that God inspires certain people to write or speak certain words, and that these words are packaged as gifts for those who read them—even years after the authors no longer walk the earth. God gave me the gift of C. S. Lewis's writing when I needed it. He opened my mind and thus massaged into my heart truth that would change me forever. It started with getting beyond my narrow perspective. As I sat down with C. S. Lewis, God moved in me. His love built me up at a time when I was weak.

If you will devote yourself to learning, you will become a better man. You will be happier and more useful. But, more importantly, if you devote yourself to learning, you will, regardless of whether you read about Martin Luther or Steve Martin, learn God's truth. All truth is God's truth, so if something is true, he is behind it. I am not saying that everything you read is true, however. We must ground ourselves in the Word of God as our foundation for truth, and we must choose carefully what we allow into our minds. If we allow that which is true to soak our minds, it will season us with God's wisdom.

Those truths are signposts, though. They are not destinations. They are markers on the journey to deeper intimacy with Jesus.

It's worthwhile to travel long and hard on the journey toward him. When you get there, take a load off and sit at his feet. You will learn from him, and learning God's truth will make you a better man.

CHAPTER 7

Forge Your Vessel

Or do you not know that your body is a temple of the Holy Spirit within you, whom you have from God? You are not your own, for you were bought with a price. So glorify God in your body.

—1 Cor. 6:19–20

L et's say you are planning to sail around the world. Let's also say your father gave you a sailboat fit for the task—at least the bare necessities. Your adventure begins in only a month. With your survival depending on this boat, you wisely devote your time to making sure it is fit to sail. So you service the outboard engine, making sure it is in peak operating condition. And you gather your gear, checking and rechecking your list, to ensure you have everything necessary for life upon the sea. Then you clean it from stem to stern. You want this boat, your ship, ready to take you on an adventure filled with danger and delight.

Our bodies are our ships for the journey of life. God gives us one body, and it is useful for the life he has prepared for us. You need a healthy vessel if you are to be strong and show yourself a man.

Too many men of God are weak, fat, lazy, and unhealthy. It seems their vessels got stranded at low tide. They sit stuck on the shore and are wasting away. Many abuse their bodies through neglect and sins of various kinds.

The opening verse of this chapter refers to sexual immorality, which is a sin committed against one's own body. It is, of course, also a sin committed against other people and God himself, but sexual immorality is self-harm. So it goes with the sins of gluttony, laziness, and drunkenness.

In our modern world of automation and engineered comfort, too many men have grown soft. Everything is easy, so why make life harder than it needs to be? Our digital world has conditioned us to ignore the physical reality in which we live. According to the National Institute of Diabetes and Digestive and Kidney Diseases, 74 percent of men are overweight or obese.[1] That is an insane statistic that speaks to the complacency of men in our culture. Distracted by their jobs and responsibilities, I believe many have literally forgotten about their bodies.

Have you seen those bumper stickers that say "0.0"? It's a kind of self-deprecating joke. While marathon runners would slap a sticker on their cars that says "26.2," the fellow with the 0.0 sticker is "boasting" about his lack of running prowess. We chuckle at this, but the message is unsettling and it reveals something deeper about us. These stickers make the statement that we don't need to run. At least not anymore. The message is that anyone proud of pushing his or her body to run over a long distance is foolish.

If you have flown on an airplane, you've heard the emergency speech. In the event of an emergency, the mask will fall down from the overhead console and hang in front of you. What's the first step after that? It's not to put your child's mask on him or her. It's not to put the old lady's mask on her. Put on your own mask first. Why? Because you can help someone only when you can breathe. In the same way, we must make sure to take care of our bodies so we can take care of others. We need to prioritize health and strength so we can serve our fellow man. It will cost money, it will take time, and it will be inconvenient—but it will be worth it.

Men are physical beings. When my daughter plays, she's tender. She has fun, but she is more careful. When my son plays, it's all speed and physicality. The trampoline becomes an octagon for wrestling. He uses our sloped driveway as a drag strip into the street. God made males to be this way, capable and interested in physical pursuits. If we are to cultivate our masculinity, we must cultivate the vessels that carry us.

STEWARDSHIP

One of my roommates in college was a genetically gifted athlete: fast, strong, and coordinated. He excelled at nearly every sport I saw him try, save golf. He was also a keen student of sports.

One night we got into an argument. "I think hard work and practice are really what separates the greats. I mean, these guys are really great because they've worked hard enough to get there. It's all about practice and hard work," I said.

"So you think if you practiced hard enough, you could make it to the Olympics in the 100 meter?" he asked.

"Well . . . uh . . ."

Of course I could never make it to the Olympics. Not everyone is blessed with that kind of body. But we are all blessed with a body, regardless of what it looks or how it performs. Some guys are built like a truck, some like a gazelle, and some like a spider. We must take the body we've been given and treat it with the kindness it deserves. We must, out of respect for the gift of the body, exercise and fuel the body with healthy foods. The body carries the mind and soul. If you are a Christ follower, it also carries the Spirit of God. The body must be maintained and improved to keep it fit for service.

Libraries are full of books on how to exercise and eat right. No one is unhealthy for lack of knowledge or money. Much of ill health is attributed to a lack of effort. Run, lift weights, kayak, play sports, swim, hike, or learn a martial art. Any activity that gets the body moving is better than nothing, but strenuous activity is the key to a strong body. Drink lots of water and not much alcohol. Eat plenty of protein. Eat fruits, nuts, and vegetables. It is not complicated.

I will say this, though. Diets do not work. This isn't merely my opinion, it's statistically true. According to Gary Foster, director of the Weight and Eating Disorders Program at the University of Pennsylvania, nearly 65 percent of people return to their pre-diet weight within three years.[2] While a rigid exercise or diet regimen may help jumpstart someone into healthful living, it is not sustainable. What is sustainable is a changed lifestyle that starts today, continues tomorrow, and never ends until we do. Caring for your vessel starts right now.

If you want to lose weight, start by getting a dog. Go to the local animal shelter, peer into the pleading eyes of one of the many pups there, and adopt one. Take her home and commit yourself to taking care of her. One of the most important aspects of caring for a dog is exercise. The dog needs a daily walk or run—and so do you. Every morning I get up with my dog, Titus, and run with him. He keeps me motivated. Our time spent together not only makes my body healthier but also my mind and my spirit. I have prayed many prayers over the spotted back of Titus during the early morning hours as we run through my neighborhood.

In college I treated my body like a monster truck. I fueled it with high octane liquids and ran it hard. I don't say this to be funny. It was ridiculous, dangerous, and foolish. Many times I could have been killed. God rescued me from several dangerous situations and soothed over some idiotic messes I created.

If you are a young man, do not think it's customary to abuse your body with alcohol, drugs, and sexual immorality. I figured it was what guys my age did, so I excused my behavior. But looking back I realize I was a poor steward of the vessel God had given me. You can do better. If you are a father of young kids, you don't have to let your waistline grow as your muscles shrink. You too may think this is normal for guys at your stage in life, but it isn't. It robs you of your manhood. It saps your energy for the good opportunities God has placed in your life. If you are a middle-aged man, you do not have to let yourself go, for you aren't old yet. Finally, if you are an older man, do not resign yourself to decomposing while you live. My father, who is in his early sixties, has in the past several years climbed a couple mountains, completed two separate overnight challenges designed to mirror stages of the selection process for Army Special Forces candidates, and run a half marathon. Glorify God in your body. He gave it to you. Use it, improve it, and enjoy it.

NOT SO FAST

Regardless of how we care for our bodies, we are destructible creatures living in a fallen world. We must remember that health is not holy in and of itself. If we believe health equates to holiness, we would immediately become unholy if we got sick or hurt. God doesn't work this way. Suffering is inevitable, and our physical bodies will give out. Sickness and injury are part of living in a fallen world.

As I write this I am frustrated by this very truth. For months I experienced outstanding health and strength. Every day I ran several miles, and three to five days a week I lifted weights and trained Brazilian jiu-jitsu. That's nearly three hours of exercise on some days. I felt like Superman. On my squat rack I keep a strip of painter's tape with my current five repetition maxes for each of my lifts. During this period I pushed through many prior records and lifted more weight.

Until now.

It started with a cold or sinus infection, something minor and annoying. One evening several days ago I stayed up late, got up very early, and failed on a set of squats. My other lifts felt weak. By noon I realized I was sick. Shortly after that, I injured my neck doing overhead presses. I am not exactly sidelined, but I'm sure not in full form.

It is clear what has happened. I believe God allowed this sickness to slay an idol of mine. As I've mentioned, I am an idol factory. As I excel physically, I get too into it. I wrap up my identity in it and then pride pops up. It is disgusting and it will not do for a man of God. Thus, my Father humbles me and reminds me I am completely dependent upon him. He reminds me that my strength, when I have it, is a gift.

Maybe you are on the opposite end of the spectrum. Maybe it's hard for you to get off the couch, and you cannot imagine making exercise an idol. Some people don't enjoy exercise, especially if they haven't done much of it. If that's you, God will still give you a dose of humility. It may be in the form of failing knees or diabetes or heart problems. Your idol of comfort or gluttony will be slain if you walk with the Lord.

Though being humbled is never fun at the time, it is an act of extreme love. I am much too blind to see the false gods I put onto the shrine of my life. Even those close to me cannot always see them. But not only is God jealous for his glory, he is jealous for his children. As his son, I have the privilege of being reminded of where my worship has turned to something other than God. Sometimes it takes an injury or illness to get my attention, and I'm good with that. I want to know when I've stepped off the path.

Men want to be self-sufficient and strong. We don't want to need anyone. Even though we really need help, we won't ask for it. Come on; we're *men*. While a measure of independence is good, we must never forget our constant dependence on God. Human life is a miracle, but we do not value it. We take our lives for granted as much as we do the drapes in the living room. We need to be reminded that we rely upon God for every waking moment.

Deathbed conversions are real, because everything is stripped away that is not grounded in reality. Many would say, "Yes, of course you called on the name of Jesus in a time like that—you had nothing else to turn to!"

Exactly.

When our bodies fail, and they will, we are brought face to face with the truth that we are like grass: here today, gone tomorrow. The man on his deathbed who gasps the name of Jesus as his last source of hope has a true epiphany. It is he who sees clearly, not those of us in the strength of our youth. Weakness makes room for the glory of God to shine, and it also puts our hearts in the state where we are ready to accept help. This is where we need to be.

Whether you are eighteen or eighty, through illness, injury, or the death of your peers, God will remind you that your physical body has an expiration date. We will break down. We should take care of it, but we should never elevate it too highly.

A WORD ABOUT INDULGENCE

Christians are not called to ascetic living (that is, foregoing all worldly pleasures in the name of holiness and purity). We are not required to live like monks and deny our bodies of all pleasure, for pleasure comes from the hand of God. Good food and good drink are gifts from God. Solomon said it this way:

> *Behold, what I have seen to be good and fitting is to eat and drink and find enjoyment in all the toil with which one toils under the sun the few days of his life that God has given him, for this is his lot. Everyone also to whom God has given wealth and possessions and power to enjoy them, and to accept his lot and rejoice in his toil—this is the gift of God.*
>
> Eccl. 5:18–19

Paul writes, "So I do not run aimlessly; I do not box as one beating the air. But I discipline my body and keep it under control, lest after preaching to others I myself should be disqualified" (1 Cor. 9:26–27). The message here is one of balance. We should enjoy God's gifts with our bodies but with moderation and wisdom. We should have the discipline to say no to that which is not honoring to God in our bodies, whether that is a second slice of pie or another glass of wine. We must also remember that our behavior affects other people and may influence them. We are not autonomous people living on an island. Others watch us and imitate what we do.

Not all aspects of asceticism are to be thrown out, however. Take fasting. Jesus endorsed fasting. But he understood a danger of self-denial: pride. Jesus warned against fasting publicly and making a show of our pious denial of self. Fasting, be it from food or coffee or beer or anything else, is a spiritual practice meant to remind us that all good gifts come from God. Our lives depend upon him. Fasting is by nature temporary, as we experience power from foregoing something and then returning to it with gladness.

I do not think many of us need to be warned against asceticism. Most of us would be wise to discipline our bodies more, especially in the matters of what we take into our bodies. Most men tend toward overindulgence, not self-deprivation.

Alcohol gladdens the heart, but it can also kill you. It can be a relaxing treat or a numbing agent. You can be drunk with wine, or you can be drunk with the Spirit (Eph. 5:18). The dangers of drinking are deadly serious for some. Solomon issues a warning:

> *Who has woe? Who has sorrow?*
> *Who has strife? Who has complaining?*
> *Who has wounds without cause?*
> *Who has redness of eyes?*
> *Those who tarry long over wine;*
> *Those who go to try mixed wine.*
> *Do not look at wine when it is red,*
> *When it sparkles in the cup*
> *And goes down smoothly.*
> *In the end it bites like a serpent*
> *And stings like an adder.*
> Prov. 23:29–32

For the person who abstains completely from drinking, he must watch that he doesn't become prideful or pass judgment on those who do not. Alcohol is neither forbidden nor encouraged for the believer, and the teetotaler is not more holy than the one who partakes. Neither should judge the other, for it is a personal choice that should be based on prayer and wisdom.

So how much alcohol is too much? If one chooses to drink, where is the threshold between God-glorifying enjoyment and sinful drunkenness? This is, of course, different for each person, and each man must decide for himself. I enjoy a drink now and then, and I can tell by feel when I need to call it quits. I have the power to do this, but some don't. If you cannot control your drinking, or your family has a history of alcoholism, you should eliminate it completely from your life. An out of control man is a dangerous thing, and he can cause all kinds of harm to himself and others.

Drinking does not make a man evil or foolish; it simply brings his evil and foolishness to the surface. It is wise to be careful with alcohol.

CULTIVATING STRENGTH

We have said a bit about diet and exercise, but now I would like to turn our attention to physical strength. This is a core component of masculinity often overlooked in Christian circles.

Just remember that some men are more blessed than others in their physical bodies. Some men are naturally strong and healthy, while others may suffer from disease or frailty. This does not make them less manly than genetically gifted men. Those who must work to overcome disease, injury, and bad genetics are very manly indeed. All who are active must at some point deal with nagging injuries. Often men return from war with missing limbs or various impairments that affect the body's ability to function fully. We cannot help what happens to our bodies in the course of living in a broken world, but we have the choice to cultivate our strength as best we're able. We must be good stewards of the body God gave us. David praises the Lord for his strength: "He trains my hands for war, so that my arms can bend a bow of bronze" (Ps. 18:34).

Physical strength is part of manhood. It does not matter that our world is increasingly automated and digital. A man should be strong. As author and strength coach Mark Rippetoe says, "Strong people are harder to kill than weak people and more useful in general."

For a man to function at his optimum, he should be as strong as possible given his body type, health, and genetics.

The body is an adaptive organism; that is, it responds to the stressors placed upon it by preparing itself to meet those stressors the next time it encounters them. When you sit in a chair for several hours, the body has no need to strengthen. In fact, the little-used muscles begin to atrophy, which hurts the posture. The posture affects all limbs and joints by holding them in their proper place: shoulders back, head up, hips forward. Sedentary habits compromise the entire system.

On the other hand, if the body is challenged through weight training, which is what I recommend, it will adapt positively. As muscles are progressively overloaded through increased weight, the body responds by rebuilding the muscles so they are ready to handle the weight. (I recommend Mark Rippetoe's program outlined in his book *Starting Strength: Basic Barbell Training*.)

A noble man of God uses his strength for good, to serve others. His strength allows him to fight in battle or help a neighbor move furniture. Getting strong is also a fundamental component of keeping his mind healthy.

Additionally, building a strong physique also builds confidence. Confident men are influential men, and if you wish to influence others, it helps to be physically fit.

Strength is a gift from God. A man should be strong and capable. He should be able to put his physical manliness to use. This is not a call to bloated buffoonery. You have seen those men who wear tiny shirts to make their arms look bigger. You have seen the men who use performance-enhancing drugs in an effort to transform into the Hulk. This is insecurity, not strength. Machismo is not manliness.

A man's strength is important, and he should cultivate it for a purpose. While athletic competition is a good thing, it is not the goal of strength. What matters most in building our bodies is that we become maximally effective and happy in the life God has prepared for us. Fitness makes us better dads, husbands, friends, and neighbors.

Build the strength of your vessel.

CHAPTER 8

Ignite the Heart

Happy is he who still loves something he loved in the nursery: He has not been broken in two by time; he is not two men, but one, and he has saved not only his soul but his life.

—G. K. Chesterton

We have learned the process a man goes through from birth to adulthood. We have examined the shipwreck caused by idolatry and the unhappy quest to find something other than God to satisfy his God-hungry soul. We have considered what it looks like to show yourself a man. We have, moving from a foundation of identity in Christ, looked at building the mind and the body.

We must now engage the heart.

People say we should "follow our heart," but given that the heart is deceitful above all things (Jer. 17:9), that might be a roadmap to disaster. If you follow a dark heart, it'll take you down dark paths, right? Maybe. It might be the trail to a summit of righteous manhood. It depends upon who owns your heart: you or Jesus. So is it good or bad to follow our hearts? Actually, it's both.

What is meant by "the heart" if not the organ? Let's allow Scripture to do the talking. Proverbs 4:23 says, "Keep your heart with all vigilance, for from it flow the springs of life." The heart of a man is the wellspring of his life. From it his emotions, thoughts, and actions flow. It is the seat of who he is. If we get the mind, we get part of the man. If we get the heart, we get all of him. God is not satisfied with a la carte relationships; he pursues the entire man, heart and all.

Many men exist with caverns in their chests. I see in them deep ruts of their worn-out routines. Get up, go to work, go home, watch television, go to sleep. Repeat. Day after day, year after year this pattern continues. The man grows numb and weary, but he trudges on. His eyes glaze. He avoids risk. Maybe retirement or that golf trip will make life better, he thinks. It doesn't. He keeps moving, unengaged from the people and world around him.

Little does he know, Satan is pleased with his numb life. The man's heart is quiet; his uprising against evil is nonexistent. He poses no danger to the Devil, as no one will follow this kind of man. He is a sleepwalker. It is easy to tempt this man because he's looking for something bright and shiny to escape his boredom. He neither fights nor cries nor pursues anything; he just survives quietly.

Honestly, sometimes that man is me. I can describe him well because I have trod his paths. It is during these times that my work gets only a shell of me. My church gets the smiling me who doesn't want to get into the gritty truth. My family? They get me in the flesh but not in the spirit. My heart is on the shelf, as I am not engaged in the present moment.

This never happened when I was a boy. My heart was ablaze for adventure and fun and new experiences. I built ramps and launched into the air on my bike. I climbed trees. Each day I rushed out my front door in a full sprint in bare feet, ready for exploits. I laughed my guts out. I was elated to be alive. I still feel this way most of the time, but sometimes I get into the drone mode. This does not have to be.

God made us to be fully alive.

Look at the men we call heroes. Some of my heroes include C. S. Lewis, Charles Spurgeon, St. Paul, and Lt. Gen. Hal Moore (Lt. Gen. Moore was the real-life protagonist in the movie *We Were Soldiers*). What is the common thread among them? Their hearts were ablaze with faith and passion. They were fire-breathing men. They kept the faith. They risked. They failed. They fought. They bled. They *lived*.

You know what I mean. It's that feeling you get when you stand up to the bully or ask a beautiful woman to be your wife. It's that thump in your chest that shoots electricity through your extremities. This is what it feels like to be a man.

OUTDOOR ADVENTURE

Have you ever peered over the edge of a canyon? Have you ever wondered if a trail that forks right or left has potential life-or-death ramifications? Have you woken up wet from dew or hooked an aggressive largemouth bass? Have you ever floated in a cold river?

The soul of a man comes alive outdoors. Legendary outdoorsman John Muir once said, "Everybody needs beauty as well as bread, places to play in and pray in, where nature may heal and give strength to body and soul alike."[1]

This is not a matter of preference. Men were not made for the indoors but to trod all over the earth, to subdue it, respect it, and enjoy it. God gave us dominion over the world. We are to play like children in the joyful spaces he made. We were made to stand under the sun, to watch a storm approach, and to jump into lakes. The heart of a man beats hard when outside, especially in adventurous pursuits.

I once stood on a mountain thousands of feet high. I peered over the edge at the straight drop down. The wind swirled around me, tugging at my clothing. It felt like it might throw me over the ledge. I lay down and tried to make myself heavy. The air left my lungs. It was a moment of delightful terror. If I could bottle that moment, I would give it to every man I meet to make sure they've tasted it.

Getting outside makes us realize how small we are. We are very,

very small, indeed. God is very, very big. Trees are bigger than we are. The wind can kill us. Water is an untamed force. The animal kingdom is wild. Spend enough time in nature, you'll learn about yourself. It will begin to kill some of your pride as your humility blooms. God will show you his greatness in nature.

Too many men today live in a world of soft skills: talking with clients, typing reports, ordering takeout. The outdoor life requires harder skills rooted in our physicality: building fires, pitching tents, shooting firearms. This is good for a man. It shakes him awake. When he gets back to his normal life, he brings with him a renewed spirit, especially if his experience has made him worship God.

Jesus often went up to the mountain to pray. He'd sneak away to pray in a garden, or take a nap in a boat. Jesus seemed to meet with his father in nature, not only because it got him away from the crowds, but because being in the wild seemed to aid his intimacy with the Father.

I like to call it concrete detox. I am a busy young father with a career and ministry and writing projects filling my time. I rush from one thing to the next. But several times a year I am able to get away from all the busyness and immerse myself in nature. When my tires crunch on gravel or I get out of earshot of car traffic, the detox process begins. I leave the phone in the truck. I quit hurrying for a moment. I tune in to the sounds of birds and inhale the scent of the earth the way God made it. It stirs my soul. It ignites my heart.

ART

Write hard and clear about what hurts.

Ernest Hemingway

Art is truth. It drags out the subconscious and sets it on the table so we can observe it. Music plunges us into a time and place. A good book possesses us. Art engages the heart.

You don't often hear it said, but art is manly. It requires courage and boldness, sweat and tears. Art requires us to engage with our passions and feelings and beliefs. It does not matter if we are listening to a favorite song or painting a masterpiece, we all engage with art. We either consume that which is created by someone else, or we put on our boots and go make something ourselves. We need both.

Pop culture has seemingly perverted the notion of real art, but it is not as bad as it seems. Art is not delicate. Art has thrived in wars and plagues; it will survive postmodern culture.

Art is not gendered, of course. It is no more masculine than it is feminine. Male artists do not create better art than female artists. The playing field is even, but the way we interact with art is different.

By and large, women do a better job of remaining in touch with their emotions; that is, the symptoms of their hearts. Men tend to minimize their emotions or act out on them in unhealthy ways. I know I do. What art does specifically for men is get them to engage with their passions and beliefs in a healthy way. It requires them to face the truth and consider their hopes.

When a man spills his guts in a creative venture, that's courage. I want to see it. When he pushes through his insecurities and creates something beautiful, I want to be alongside him. It could be anything: a carving, a logo, a shirt, a barbeque pit, or a song. It does not matter. When we plumb the depths of our souls and allow others to see them, we are reflecting the essence of our creative Creator. We are showing the world what men really are: the *imago dei*.

God made people in his image. Though broken, all of us show the world different attributes of God. Whether we are believers or atheists, we reflect his glory, nonetheless. Our uniqueness reflects the creativity and brilliance of God.

If you want to know more about yourself, try making something. As you struggle to create something, you will draw out parts of yourself you didn't know existed. You will show up in what you create; we show what we're made of. When we show what we're made of, we show the world about God because he made us. In fact, God is *in us*. Christians are a dwelling place for the Spirit of God, and he will provide his cosmic assistance in our creative endeavors.

Art is reflective of the divine because we are reflective of the divine. When we extract ourselves through an artistic adventure, we will offer a portal for other people to see God. I'll be real with you, though: the portal might be forged through your pain. You might write about your journey through the darkness of grief or abuse. You might sing about your rejection. But if you do anything, do what is true and real. It doesn't have to be perfect; it just needs to be honest.

When we broadcast truth through art, we push back darkness by bringing light into the world. The truth of art pushes back darkness and glorifies God because God's story is perfect. If the excruciating is included in the artist's story, it is part of a beautiful story. It may not be a shining moment, but it's a scene in God's grand narrative. Art makes life beautiful by showing scenes from God's story.

For some, pursuing art is cathartic. When I write, it untangles my thoughts. It feels good. But pain is also involved in the struggle. That's a normal part of the process. Over time, I have learned to make friends with the discomfort because I can feel the Spirit of God moving through me. I am doing something God has validated. It's not about the end result, about the sales or the affirmation. It's about dancing the dance with my Maker. It's about opening myself to him and putting what's inside out there. It's about the process. I cringe when I read what I wrote a year ago, but I cringe more thinking about who I'd be if I had not written it.

You may think art is for the creative types. I agree. But what you may not have learned about yourself is that you are, by design, a creative type. The eminently creative God of the universe has imprinted himself upon you. One of his communicable attributes—those attributes he shares with us—is creativity. Explore what that might mean for you and don't give way to insecurity or self-doubt. Do not listen to the lies of Satan, which will immediately rise to counter your creativity. Just give it a shot. Build a table, write an article, or paint a picture of your dog.

All men should pursue an art. It will make them better men, and it will beautify the world with God's majesty. It will also stir their hearts.

BEING WHERE YOU ARE

God did not call you to live tomorrow right now. He does not ask that we relive our past. God has put you right here, right now. Unfortunately, I almost never believe this.

Our hearts are never alive when we are outside of the moment. When we are living in our heads instead of our current moment, we are actually nowhere. We are neither here nor there. This is why I have often abandoned my family in the evenings, even though I am physically present. I have a project or meeting on my mind, thus I'm not present with my wife and children. They deserve better.

My Uncle Don gets this. I call him Unc. If you ever meet Unc, you will know what I mean. He stares at you with his electric blue eyes. As you talk, he listens and then pauses before speaking. He typically exhales then responds, engaged deeply in what's on your mind. He can switch from talking about horsepower to a broken marriage and back without hesitation. He goes deep and shallow. He is *present*. The best conversations are between two present people. Engaged in conversation with each other, the two will go deep. It will be rich, of substance. It will bring the heart into the present moment.

Our busyness kills our presence. If we don't actively control our calendars, they can kill our presence. When we say yes, yes, yes to everything asked of us, we pile obligation upon ourselves. And, frankly, we think we're more important than we actually are. Take the burned-out pastor. With a heart for God and other people, he works himself to exhaustion. If he meets with everyone who asks of him, he'll have no time to study or respond to other people with equal or more pressing needs. Why does he do this? He thinks he's the linchpin. He thinks if he doesn't do all of the shepherding, it won't get done. But he needs to understand and trust that God will get done what God wants done. He does not require, or even depend on, his children to do all of his bidding for him.

The strength of a man is like the sun under a magnifying class. Dispersed broadly, sunlight provides benefit to all around. But when it's concentrated, as it is when a man is present and engaged, it wields tremendous power.

Be where you are.

BOYS AT HEART

G. K. Chesterton said we are blessed when we do not lose that which we have loved our entire lives: "Happy is he who still loves something he loved in the nursery." When we grow up, we are encouraged to throw off our childish ways. In many respects, this is good. We should give up our tantrums and our endless selfishness. We should eat with better manners and think before we speak. Sure, we should grow up.

But what about the exhilaration we once felt at play? What about the reckless abandon with which we once lived life? Each day was a gift to make the best of. A stick was a gun, and a ball became a device in a newly created combat sport. We drew pictures and ate pizza and ran until our hair was soaked with sweat. What happened to the spirit of these boys?

These little boys are alive within us. Unlike the butterfly that sheds its cocoon and morphs into a new creature, a man does not shed his boyhood. He keeps it suppressed, but the heart of the boy is also the heart of the man. Remember Jesus's words in Mark 10:15: "Truly, I say to you, whoever does not receive the kingdom of God like a child shall not enter it."

How does a child receive something of great value? Their eyes gleam and their faces beam. They will not shut up about it. They can't sit still. Think of a kid on Christmas morning, running around the house on cloud nine. Let me ask you: do you miss that excitement?

Kids lack the ability to quiet the longings of their hearts. Adults lack the ability to bring the longings out. Especially men. But this does not have to be so. You see, for a man to embrace his manhood, for him to show himself a man, he must take life as a child. He must receive God like a child receives his father. He must live in God's kingdom the way a child runs around the Christmas tree. And just how can a man retrieve his childlikeness? How can he get back the youthful passion and zeal for life?

No prescription for childlikeness exists, but we can get our boy-ish hearts back. The solution is one word: play. We must learn to play again, to let ourselves laugh and get dirty and roughhouse. That's what boys do. As men grow, they become a bit too serious. They take themselves too seriously. I know I have. Play resurrects the heart of the boy. So whether your version of play is climbing a mountain, jamming on a guitar, or playing golf, learn to play again. Have fun for the sake of having fun. That's what boys do.

Life is short, but it goes on forever after we die. On the mortal side of things, we have a very short window of time. If we are to show ourselves as men, we must ignite our hearts. We must cultivate them, care for them, and do the things that make us feel *alive*.

Awaken your heart, brother!

CHAPTER 9

The Gentleman Savage

And one of the elders said to me, "Weep no more; behold, the Lion of
the tribe of Judah, the Root of David, has conquered, so that he can
open the scroll and its seven seals." And between the throne and the
four living creatures and among the elders I saw a Lamb standing,
as though it had been slain, with seven horns and with seven eyes,
which are the seven spirits of God sent out into all the earth.

—Rev. 5:5–6

Beauty can be complex. In fact, beauty can be formed by a contrast of opposites. Often when you have what seem to be diametrically opposed qualities, you have the ingredients of beauty. Contrast forms a beautiful picture.

A blazing orange sunrise is made all the more beautiful because it rises against a horizon. The sun beautifies the horizon, and the horizon beautifies the sunrise, culminating in a masterpiece. The contrast makes it so. If the sun were to rise against a blazing orange horizon, the sunrise would be concealed, washed away without the complexity of contrast. You would also not notice the horizon, hills, mountains, and trees against which the sun rises. Contrast helps frame the excellence of this beautiful daily event.

President Theodore Roosevelt once said, "Speak softly and carry a big stick." He was referring to his foreign policy of showing strength without bravado. *Be strong, yet humble.* This is a theory of contrasts. These two opposing values combine to create a wise approach.

If we are to show ourselves as men, we must look to our ultimate example. Who was the greatest man who ever lived? Jesus, who was the perfect representation of a man. He was full of power, righteousness, and mercy. He was a true man. He was the God-man.

We must not look to him merely to emulate him as a good example, but we men should look to Jesus as the object of our worship. Imitation is fine, but worship is the aim. Putting worship first works well because as we worship Jesus, we will, over time, transform ourselves to be more like him. Worship is transformative, for we become what we behold. In other words, we start the process of becoming what we love the most: "And we all, with unveiled face, beholding the glory of the Lord, are being transformed into the same image from one degree of glory to another. For this comes from the Lord who is the Spirit" (2 Cor. 3:18).

If we look to Jesus as our example and our Savior worthy of all worship, let's ask: What is he like? What virtues did he display? How did Jesus show himself a man?

For starters, he was the only perfect man in history. When he came to earth, he came as fully God and fully man. This is the first dichotomy of Jesus. He was powerful as God, yet he allowed himself to be limited as a man. He laid down some of his divinity to become fully human (Phil. 2:6). As he put off some of his godliness, he did not cease to be God. If this confuses you, do not worry about it. It is a beautiful mystery. It is cosmic art. In Jesus you have a marriage of the immortal with the mortal; you have a joining of the divine and the human.

You have the lion and the lamb. This is the second dichotomy of Jesus.

In his 1986 sermon on Palm Sunday, John Piper explains, "The principle that I am trying to illustrate and that makes Christ stand out as absolutely unique is this: beauty or excellence consists in the right proportion of diverse qualities."[1]

Consider the male lion. He is one of the most majestic creatures in all of the earth. He is stout. His muscles ripple with every move. He is respected by other animals, as he is a masterpiece of potential violence. No animal wants to pick a fight with him. His powerful roar travels for miles, making the hair stand up on the hearers' necks. The lion is an apex predator, seated comfortably at the top of the wild food chain. He is not hunted; he is the hunter. The lion is wild and untamed. He is the *king*.

The lamb, on the other hand, is the opposite of the lion. It is meek and helpless; tender, small, and vulnerable. The lamb is prey. When shorn, it appears naked and sad. While the primary attribute of the lion is his ferocity, the lamb's is its innocence.

Jesus is both lion and lamb. In Revelation 5, he is referred to as a slain lamb, further reinforcing the contrast: a living lion and a slain lamb. Jesus is the most powerful King, yet he is also a living sacrifice. He is utterly perfect in this dichotomy of character. His contrast of meekness and dominance is beautiful.

I believe all of us should do our best to be like Jesus, the perfect One. And that is hard to do. It is impossible, actually. But over time, by beholding his glory—by worshiping him for who he is—we will be more like him.

If we are to pursue Jesus as the object of our worship and strive to imitate him as the ideal man, we must do something with this lion and lamb dichotomy. Frankly, I find it difficult to apply the lion and the lamb theory directly to my life and my masculinity. I find it difficult to transpose these qualities to myself. In fact, I'm not sure we're even supposed to. We need another way to relate to this theory.

I propose that as men we strive to be a *gentleman savage*.

When you combine the qualities of a gentleman (dignity, kindness, humility, and respect) with the attributes of a savage (ferocity, courage, physicality, and a warrior spirit), you have a whole man. There is a reason I do not call this archetype a *savage gentleman*. That is because, as I believe Christ would have it, the gentle qualities must come first. Scripture predominantly shows Jesus as gentle and merciful, but, of course, we also see his savage nature. For example, when he clears the temple with the flailing whip, flipping tables, and tearing through the place, he does so *out of love*. He drove out men making a mockery of his Father's house because he loves his Father too much to let that continue. From this event we learn any violence of action must be rooted in love and born out of compassion. Gentleness comes first. Love must always come first.

The man who is only a gentleman may be weak. The man who is only a savage may be a bloodthirsty warmonger. Clearly Jesus was neither of these. He was a perfect blend of ferocity and tenderness. We too may seek to blend these qualities.

Let us explore this concept further.

ABILITY TO FIGHT

I've never been much of a fighter. Growing up, I had a few scraps here and there, but for the most part I was a very peaceful kid who tried to avoid fights, even through my adolescent and teen years. It still holds true today.

When I was in college, a moment in time changed me as a man, though I had no idea at the time. My buddies and I went to a bar. This particular evening, my girlfriend, who later became my wife, came with us. In fact, she drove us in her Jeep. Of course, there was excessive drinking for all involved except sweet Lindsay. We showed up drunk and got drunker when we got to the bar. (I still wonder why she stayed with me.)

As we stood around with music blaring and smoke wafting, things went bad. Someone threw a quarter and hit my friend Daniel in the face with it. (This is what happens when you hang out in these kinds of places.) Of course, we should've just let it go, but we didn't. We asked around about who threw the quarter. I am not sure why we wanted to know. Eventually, we found a group of guys who were happy to claim responsibility. They were drunker than we were and pretty angry.

These guys were clearly looking for a fight. They became belliger-
ent and started toward my friend. It was at this point that we tried to
diffuse the situation. I offered to buy the guys a round, but it seemed
they wanted to fight.

Someone told the bouncer, who approached the gathering crowd
and forcibly removed these aggressive guys from the bar. As the stocky
bouncer dragged them out, they shot menacing looks at us.

Lindsay understandably had had enough. She demanded we leave
the bar. We complied, and our ears rang from the overloud music
when we stepped out of the bar and into the quiet night.

We had parked in the alley behind the bar. As we walked to Lindsay's Jeep, we noticed some guys walking in front of us. It was them.
We had not waited inside the bar long enough for them to leave. They
quickly turned around and confronted us.

I stood toe to toe with the main instigator, and my buddy Daniel
faced a tall member of their group, who looked down at Daniel. In the
distance I spotted one of their friends reaching underneath the seat of
his heavy-duty Ford. For what, I didn't know. My guy began to berate
me, sticking his finger in my face and slurring that he was going to
knock me out. Everything slowed down. To my right were Lindsay
and her Jeep. To my left was Daniel. In front of us were these guys
aching for a fight. I considered the situation and intuitively figured it
was best not to throw a punch. After some words and what felt like a
lengthy standoff, we parted and left the scene.

But I was shaking.

When we got to our dorm, my adrenaline had spiked. Now I
wished that they were here. I had changed my mind and now wanted
to fight, but no fight was to be had. It was a pathetic situation, now
that I think about it. We should never have gone to the bar, and we
should never have searched for the quarter thrower. It certainly was
foolish to get mad once I got home. God had delivered two groups
of drunken idiots (excluding Lindsay) from an alley brawl. Who
knows what could have happened? I should have praised God and
gone to bed.

This is a rather unremarkable and stupid story, except that it reveals something significant about all of us men. The reason I was so rattled by this juvenile incident at the bar was that I feared the unknown. I was not sure if I would've won or lost the fight, and I wanted to know. A fight was an alien thing to me. It scared me. This fear nearly compelled me to throw a punch that would have started a dangerous brawl. This incident was a seed that would later germinate in my life.

Several months ago I began training in Brazilian jiu-jitsu. I had never trained in any martial art, so I thought I would give it a try. Brazilian jiu-jitsu is a beautiful martial art, and I quickly recognized the value of it. I also immediately realized that I was not tough. I have sparred (called "rolling") with black belts and MMA fighters, most of them smaller than I am. They have all humbled me. It doesn't take long for a trained fighter to get you into a bad position, trust me. I am a low-level white belt still learning the ropes, but something has changed in me. In fact, it happened the first time I rolled.

My fear of the fight vanished.

It's not because I realized I'm a good fighter. It removed the mystery of physical combat. I had no idea until I started training Brazilian jiu-jitsu that I had been scared to fight. In fact, most fights result because of fear. Out of fear of embarrassment, someone feels the need to prove himself. Usually, he wants to test his manhood.

Now that I have a measure of training, I am even less inclined to fight. Street fights are nasty, stupid, and dangerous. If I were to relive that ridiculous situation in the alley again, I would have done what I could to avoid the confrontation, hustled Daniel and Lindsay into the Jeep, and left immediately. I would have done so without shaking.

You're probably wondering what this has to do with biblical manhood.

If we are to be men of virtue, we must control ourselves. If we are to control ourselves, we must know how to handle ourselves physically. If we know how to handle ourselves physically, we will be calmer and less anxious men and more effective in life. Not everyone needs to train to fight. But it doesn't hurt to have the skill. Training to fight can make a more peaceful man. The best fighters at my gym are respectful and laid-back. They are peaceful warriors.

Regardless of whether you train in martial arts, you need an outlet for your aggression and a sport to hone your physicality. You need a way to test yourself. In the late 1800s, churches in Britain began to understand the value of masculine physicality. A movement began called Muscular Christianity. The movement promoted sports and physical living, which was countercultural to the Victorian culture of the day. This movement eventually birthed the YMCA, and its impact is still felt today. Aside from the Muscular Christianity movement, the church has largely ignored the importance of physical fitness and preparedness.

One of the vital roles of manhood is to protect those who cannot protect themselves. We must be able to apply force when needed. I don't mean punching someone in the mouth because he looked at your wife. I mean legitimate defense of the defenseless, which is an act of sacrificial love. Of course, we have the police and military for much of this. But not all of it. Those brave men and women of the police and military cannot be everywhere at all times. Sometimes a man needs to act, albeit in love.

I believe that through preparation and training, a man will become more peaceful. An untested man is an unsure man. In the college incident, I was an unsure man. If training to fight makes me more peaceful, and peacefulness is a fruit of the Spirit, then I will train to fight.

Paul says, "But the fruit of the Spirit is love, joy, peace, patience, kindness, goodness, faithfulness, gentleness, self-control; against such things there is no law" (Gal. 5:22–23). Choosing the peaceful solution when you are capable of violence is noble. When a strong man deals gently with others, it demonstrates his character. His strength affords him the option of peace because he is not intimidated. The weak and untrained man, on the other hand, may choose peace not because he is peaceful but because he is afraid of conflict. The way of the godly warrior is to be capable of violence but a lover of peace—and a lover of others.

The gentleman savage is able and willing to put his strength to use in the service of others. He avoids violence, but he is capable of standing up for others if called upon, for he is driven by love.

BENEVOLENT DIGNITY

Shortly before Donald Trump was elected president, audio was leaked of him talking crudely about women. Many responded in defense of then-candidate Trump by saying it was just common locker-room talk. *All men talk like that*, they said.

Actually, they don't.

Godly men are not prudes, but neither are they vulgar. I get the sense that Jesus was a lot of fun to be around. The more time I spend following him, the more I know this is true. He is wild and dangerous. He is unpredictable in the right ways. But Jesus has a benevolent dignity about him. He is respectful and considerate of others. He is kind to the lowly.

It is manly to clothe yourself with dignity and self-control, like Jesus. It is manly to be gentle and kind. At the root of all of this is a spirit of putting others first. That is what being a gentleman is about.

Male culture does not need to be filled with vulgarity. In fact, it should not be. Paul tells the Ephesians, "Let there be no filthiness nor foolish talk nor crude joking, which are out of place, but instead let there be thanksgiving" (5:4).

This is not about being a good little Christian boy and keeping your mouth clean. It is not about saying the right things or looking a certain way or presenting a spotless image to the world. Paul admonishes us to live a life of dignity. Foolish talk and crude joking can make others feel uncomfortable. Further, irreverent words can remove the seriousness around sacred matters. If, for example, we joke crudely about sex, we devalue it. If we are crude, we are disrespectful. This is not manly.

If God were to take all of my crude joking and foolish talk and present it to me all at once, I am sure that I would not be able to take it. It would be too much to handle. Words are powerful, and the wrong kind of words can spread darkness.

We will not be men of kindness and dignity simply by willing ourselves to be so. It requires a heart change. When a man is saved by Jesus, he gives the man a heart of flesh. The man becomes a dwelling place for the Spirit of God. He is changed from the inside out. Any effort to change without a new heart is an attempt to change from the outside in. We try to clean ourselves on the outside, but we are still foul on the inside (Matt. 23:26). The purifying grace of Christ is the source of virtue. It starts on the inside. Christ-like virtue isn't rooted in dogma or a code of honor; it's rooted in a heart that has reordered loves. Jesus does this work in a man, and he makes an ambassador out of him. As ambassadors, we must remember that our words and conduct are not merely personal choices. They impact other people and reflect the one who sent us.

God calls us salt and light in the world. Paul says in Colossians, "Let your speech always be gracious, seasoned with salt, so that you may know how you ought to answer each person" (4:6). The imagery of seasoning with salt is helpful. Salt enhances the flavors of food, and it is a preservative. Salt should not be dumped on top of food but sprinkled discriminately, depending upon each person's taste. As we seek to be men under the kingship of Jesus, we should consider how to season our conduct and our words with his salt.

We have encountered extremes of this continuum: the profane man and the judgmental prude. Jesus, of course, was neither of these. Instead, he demonstrated perfect dignity in all situations. Even when he flipped over the tables in the temple . . . rather, *especially* when he flipped over the tables in the temple, he showed dignity and righteousness.

Dignity is not about building your reputation. Though it is good to be respectful and kind to others, our motivation should come from beyond the face value of our actions. It is ultimately about being a good ambassador for Christ.

OUR GUIDING LIGHT

If the idea of a gentleman savage is helpful to you, use it. If not, throw it out. The concept of a gentleman savage is intended to help you imitate Christ as the lion and the lamb. Truth be told, it is nearly impossible to fully describe the way Jesus was a man. He was, and is, mysterious. He is better and purer than we can comprehend, much less describe. But he did not leave us in blind confusion. When Jesus ascended into heaven, the Spirit descended into his followers. Further, we have the God-inspired book of Scripture to guide us.

Numerous verses in the Bible help provide a framework for our behavior as believing men. It is important for us to understand the metanarrative of Scripture rather than to cherry pick verses from which to glean wisdom for a living. We need to know the story to know the context. The wisdom of Scripture comes from the story of redemption in Christ. Jesus's story is a true epic, not a self-help book.

Everything about our manhood should be subservient to the Word of God. We must sit underneath it, but to do that we must know what it says. And if we know what it says, we are wise to trust God and seek to walk in his ways. We must trust that the words in this ancient book are for us today. Right here, right now.

God does not demand that we become scholars in theology. It is not about rote memorization or doctrine or any ideas created by man. What we must seek is God himself as revealed through the narrative of Jesus Christ on every page of the Bible.

Nothing contributes more to our manhood than being soaked in the Word of the Lion and the Lamb.

CHAPTER 10

Building Disruption

We need you to make a ruckus.
—Seth Godin

Hans Luther wanted a better life for his son. Mining was hard on Hans, and he hoped his boy would become a lawyer, which seemed a much better path for the lad. It pleased Hans when his son enrolled at the University of Erfurt in Germany to pursue his Master of Arts. All was on the right track.

That is, until the storm.

As a miner, Hans had probably taught his son about the patron saint of miners, St. Anne. He may have even taught his son that he could pray to her. It was clearly in the back of his son's mind, for when the young man was caught in a terrible storm, he cried out to St. Anne for help: "Save me, St. Anne, and I'll become a monk!"

The storm calmed. And the young man kept his promise. But being a monk did not provide the answers he sought. However, he did find answers in his deep study of Scripture, which spoke to the importance of faith, not ritual or religion. The realization that Scripture addressed the necessity and sufficiency of faith alone as the means to salvation was a scandalous epiphany. Salvation, the young monk learned from the Bible, is not about patron saints or performance; it's about the centrality of Christ. Faith is the only way to him.

A few years later, Pope Leo X was working on a building campaign for a new church. He decided his fundraising method would be to sell indulgences, assurances of salvation guaranteed by the Catholic Church. In other words, one could buy their way to heaven.

Our young man, who was now thirty-four, could take the heresy no longer. The idea of buying salvation infuriated him. Having learned in the Bible the truth about salvation, the monk saw indulgences as offensive to God; therefore, he determined to do something about the sacrilege, which would change the course of history. He wrote a scathing assessment of the Catholic Church and its sale of indulgences, complete with ninety-five bullet points, and nailed it to the front door of the Castle Church in Wittenburg, Germany.

The young man's name: Martin Luther.[1]

Luther created a global ruckus. The Catholic Church tried to excommunicate Luther, deeming him a heretic. To escape certain death, he went on the run, holed up in a safe house, and translated the New Testament into German so more people could read Scripture and thus learn about the salvation of Jesus through faith. His ruckus started the Lutheran Church, which set into motion the Protestant Reformation.

Luther, born of peasant lineage, was one man. He was enough to make a world-changing ruckus.

In your quest to show yourself a man, you need to become comfortable making a ruckus. Walking with Jesus requires disruptive living. Jesus was a revolutionary, loved and hated by many but ignored by none. If we follow him, we're choosing the winning side in the cosmic battle of good and evil. When we step over the line in the sand and join the family of God, we had better prepare for battle. Enemies are made and battle lines are drawn.

Grab your sword and let's go.

LIVING WEIRDLY

Once you have tasted the sweetness of life with Jesus, everything else tastes a little bitter. Money, power, and the other idols we've built start to lose their luster. We will probably keep chasing idols for a time, but, eventually (after experiencing enough disappointment), we will realize that nothing compares to Jesus. We will learn to forsake everything for more time with him. This is disruptive to those who don't know Jesus. It unsettles them.

Followers of Jesus live differently. They vote with their time and money in ways that baffle others. It's not that they're perfect. Lord knows they aren't. But they are different in ways that go against culture and the norm.

A guy once told me, "I knew there was something weird about you," when he found out I was a Christian. We had worked together for months when someone gave him a copy of a book I had written, which outed me as a believer. He was actually complimenting me when he said this. The disruptive nature of my life was clear to him. It's not that I was a stainless saint; but I was different.

When faithful men act like men, their families become unique. Their homes are Christ-saturated, and from this saturation flows a different way of living.

When godly men raise children, they send flights of arrows into the world:

> *Like arrows in the hand of a warrior*
> *are the children of one's youth.*
> *Blessed is the man*
> *who fills his quiver with them!*
> Ps. 127:4–5

Something is markedly different about an authentic Christian household. The home takes on the personality of the husband and wife. If they are hospitable, open, and generous, their home will throb with love. If they value God and other people, their weird love will explode out the front door when they get their mail. Godly men cultivate weird families.

Stephen Mansfield says that manly men "tend their fields,"[2] meaning that they take inventory of the responsibilities God has granted them: friends, family, work, church, home. This is his field to grow and nourish. He takes measures to care for his field. He does not allow weeds to choke his field. He does not let thieves steal the harvest. He tends to his field.

This is, unfortunately, countercultural. Statistics show that men are moving away from presence in the home and church. The majority of men are not engaged in their work. So a man who is present, accounted for, and bold is a rare bird today. He is weird in a very, very good way.

When I have been around people of fame or fortune, it strikes me how average they really are. Most of them do not carry their stage aura with them to get a hamburger or to sled with their kids. Fame and fortune don't make extraordinary people. But I am moved when I have met men who, by virtue of their faith, walk deeply with God. Without saying a word I can feel something different emanating from them. When they enter a room, the air changes.

This is what it feels like to others when you show yourself a man.

Godly men carry hope that sets them apart from others (1 Peter 3:15). It makes others uncomfortable in a good way. *What is with this guy?* Their hope in Christ cuts their tethers to the trappings of this world. It's like they are aliens of the best kind.

This is why the unbelieving world likes to see men of faith fall. *Ha! They're human!* Of course they're human. Many well-known men of faith would do well to remind people of that instead of masquerading as an anointed prophet or demigod. It is not the man who exudes the aura, but the God who animates him.

THE SCANDAL OF WORDS

Godly men use their words wisely. Words are powerful. They are permanent and etch into the minds of listeners. When I was in middle school, a group of kids called me an oddball. I forgave them, but I couldn't forget it. It embarrassed me and wounded me. On the contrary, I will never forget the wise words of my mom before I married Lindsay. Even though she was very sad about my moving several hours away, she charged me to go. Her selfless words were wise and loving . . . and unforgettable. Words are like barbed hooks: they sink in and are hard to remove.

Here's the thing. It's not cool or popular to talk about Jesus. Surely you know this. He is, by nature, scandalous. Throughout history many have perverted his name and used him as a profit center or a whip, making him highly controversial. So when his name is mentioned to nonbelievers, they typically turn cool. Showing yourself a man means opening your mouth to share the grace of Christ no matter the consequences. It also means living your life in such a way that others catch a glimpse, though imperfect, of the real Jesus.

Romans 10:14 says, "How then will they call on him in whom they have not believed? And how are they to believe in him of whom they have never heard?" This doesn't mean proselytizing everywhere you go; rather, it's about being a man who is concerned with the truth. About being a man who is willing to share his story of redemption. About a man who will throw someone an eternal life preserver instead of worrying about being cool. It's about talking about Jesus.

The name of Jesus is powerful, and the mere utterance of it is disruptive. It brings the truth to a boil. It is like shining a light in the dark. Evil lurks just beyond the light. The demons wail when Jesus is proclaimed.

To be a good disrupter, a man must learn to use his words well. He doesn't need to be Shakespeare, but he must be capable with words. In war, orders are given in words. In the pulpit, the good news is proclaimed in the form of words. In the everyday trenches of life, words are the high and low points.

Brevity is underrated. Fearing our words might not be the right ones, many of us are prone to use too many of them. We try to broadcast a wide swath of verbal seed. But real strength lies not in speaking many words but in speaking the right ones. Jesus was a master at this. Real persuasion comes from powerful proclamation of the simple truths, not stringing big words together. This too is disruptive.

What Jesus chose not to say made a greater impact on his hearers than what he did say. Peter Drucker once said, "The most important thing in communication is hearing what isn't said." Jesus said many brilliant things, but we must hear what he chose not to say. So too, as men of God, we must communicate with what we say and what we don't. When we choose not to engage in gossip, we speak with our silence. When we pause for the right word, we speak with carefulness. When we use restraint in our words, the gaps between them speak to propriety.

Some men are talkers and some are not. That's fine. But our words are of great significance, so we must choose and use them wisely. We must allow them to disrupt. Our aim should be the glorification of Christ, and our intention should be rooted in love. If we carry noble intentions, our words might disrupt someone away from darkness and into God's light.

SHOCKING LOVE

Though we have established that physical strength is important, the mark of a Christian man is not strength; it is love. The two are complementary, but if only one is present, it must be love, a sincere love. Though sometimes love is a choice—a verb—our goal is for a heart soaked with love and affection for others.

When we exude the love of Christ as we go through our day, it will stand out. The love of Christ is not interested in reciprocity; that is, we don't give love to get love. So when you love in the coffee shop and in traffic and at work, people might raise their eyebrows. *What does he want from me?* It doesn't make sense to our contractual, tit-for-tat world.

To love people who are unlovable is bizarre and counter-intuitive to those who have not themselves been loved even when unlovable. Sadly, this is the case for far too many people. They have been loved based on their merit, or what they do . . . or perhaps not at all. It is heartbreaking. Those of us who've tasted the Scandalous Grace are to show others the nonsensical delight of love without strings.

The godly man must taste grace first before he can offer it to others. If he has met Christ, he has tasted it. And he must taste it again and again. And again. The more he drinks of grace, the more he can offer others. And, thus, the more he'll disrupt their lives with love.

Jesus said,

> You have heard that it was said, "An eye for an eye and a tooth for a tooth." But I say to you, Do not resist the one who is evil. But if anyone slaps you on the right cheek, turn to him the other also. And if anyone would sue you and take your tunic, let him have your cloak as well. And if anyone forces you to go one mile, go with him two miles.
>
> Matt. 5:38–41

This seems un-American. We are used to fair play. You invade our country, we respond with a greater force and invade yours. Japan's eventual repayment for the attack on Pearl Harbor was Hiroshima and Nagasaki. It has been reinforced in our culture that Americans should stand up for themselves. This is probably due to our scrappy pioneer heritage, and while some aspects of this thinking are good, when applied to our lives, we can easily take this idea too far. Unless we are informed and changed by Jesus's words of peace, we'll try to defend every slight and lash back at every insult. If we go around like little judges ready to set things right, we'll be angry and defensive men. This, of course, is not godly or manly.

I am not advocating the other extreme: being a pushover. I am not suggesting we teach our young men to look at the ground as the bully throws the contents of their lockers onto the hallway floor. There is a time to punch someone square in the face, to fight, but these instances are rare.

Often our aggression is not rooted in righteous protection of the innocent or legitimate self-defense. Usually we have opportunities to de-escalate and walk away, whether the conflict is potentially physical or merely verbal. If we are able to make peace out of a potentially volatile situation, we reflect Jesus well. And we will be glad we did after the fact.

We are called to be peacemakers.

Jesus's reference in the above verse about an eye for an eye is a situation much different from the rare call for righteous aggression. It is about a disposition absent of defensiveness and excessive pride.

Being proud of your family, your state, and your country is not a bad thing. Because the wrong kind of pride is sin, we Christians have made the word analogous to *egomania*. But it is not. You can be proud of the military unit you served with and proud of your daughter as she flawlessly executes her piece at her piano recital. You should be proud. But excessive pride—which is actually not pride but fear-based insecurity—comes before destruction (Prov. 16:18).

Excessive pride breeds hatred of others. If I knock you down, then I'll be higher than you. Excessive pride (again, it is merely insecurity masked in egomania) makes a man intensely sensitive. He does not know who he is, so he is scared of what he might be, and what he might not be. He does not realize the humility and the dignity of being a person made in God's image, so he will fight to create his own persona. I know a guy so sensitive that a subtle and unintentional inference about him will set him into a tailspin. He'll stew for weeks if he's slighted. The Pharisees were like this.

If we know who we are and are secure in that, according to Psalm 16, we have a beautiful inheritance, and we should be men of peace. We are privileged people. Thus, when reviled or gossiped about, we can just let it go. When we face irrational attacks from others, we can do more than keep under control, we can return hate with love.

Turning the cheek is the ultimate act of strength, but it must be rooted in humility for it to work. If we turn the cheek in a haughty manner—*you're not worth it*—we do no good to the fellow. We want to be disruptive, remember? We want to return an assault with disarming love. We want to freak out people with a heartfelt respect for them, especially when they don't deserve it. Jesus is our example when he prayed for the men who murdered him.

Jesus meets us when we are still in opposition to him, when we are traitors. He meets us in our sinful bender. We do not scale the white marble stairs to meet him; he shows up and meets us on a Thursday morning right after we ignore the homeless man, steal a parking spot, and then gawk at the waitress as she refills our coffee. Paul was busy persecuting Christians when Jesus showed up for him. Paul was a traitor. Jesus turned the other cheek, saved Paul from himself, and spun Paul's life in a beautiful direction. And he didn't just turn the other cheek; he laid down his life for Paul.

Restraint is mature, but sacrificial love is divine. It is love in spite of all faults and affronts. It is a love never afraid to speak up, never afraid to man up, and never neglecting to show up. If you want to show yourself a man, love people hard. If you want to love people hard, you'll need to be loved. Lucky for you, Jesus doles out his love lavishly. He spilled his blood as a testament to his love, and he'll meet you where you are so you can meet others where they are. And just where are we? We are all in a place of dire need of the kind of love only Jesus provides.

BUILDING DISRUPTIVE PLATFORMS

In 2006, Blake Mycoskie, a thirty-year-old guy from Arlington, Texas, took some time off from work. As a busy entrepreneur, he had a lot going on at the time, but he took the vacation. His goal was to immerse himself in the Argentinian culture. He tangoed, drank Malbec, and played polo. He even wore a pair of *alpargatas*, a soft canvas shoe popular in Argentina.

He met an American woman in a café who was working on a shoe drive. Unfamiliar with a shoe drive, Mycoskie asked her to explain it. She said that many kids in Argentina are shoeless, which makes it hard to attend school and fetch water from wells. It also contributes to illness.

Intrigued, Mycoskie visited these shoeless children. He saw their blisters and infections. He saw their pain. And it moved him. He had to do something. Should he start a charity? How could he help? A business-minded man, he considered various ideas. He became a man on a mission.

Mycoskie had an epiphany. He told an Argentinian friend, "I'm going to start a shoe company that makes a new kind of *alpargata*. And for every pair I sell, I'm going to give a pair of new shoes to a child in need."[3]

He did what he determined to do and started the company called TOMS. The business model of TOMS is relatively simple. For every pair of shoes they sell, they donate a pair to someone in need. This was a revolutionary concept at the time, and it birthed a social entrepreneurship trend called "One for one": sell one pair and give one pair away.

In an interview with Business Insider, Mycoskie explains his approach:

> *One thing that I think has become really clear is we didn't start a company with a mission, but we had a mission that turned into a company.*
>
> *And I think that's a really important distinction because I started TOMS basically to fund the giving that I wanted to do to the children I met in South America. I didn't want to start a charity to be dependent on donations.*
>
> *A lot of people now call it social enterprise, conscious capitalism, and there's a lot of labels for what we are. But I think the phrase that "we are a mission with a company" is probably the best way to describe it as opposed to a company that has a mission.*[4]

TOMS disrupted the business world. It put shoes on kids in need and provided jobs.

It caused a ruckus.

The world needs disruptive churches, businesses, and charities. It needs disruptive men to build them. It needs platforms of change that mobilize people to do the work of proclaiming the truth, feeding the hungry, and creating value in the business world.

Not everyone is called to be a Blake Mycoskie. Some are called to be disruptive accountants. That is not only legitimate, it is subversive—in a good way. To go throughout our ordinary lives with a Spirit-drenched mind-set takes courage. When ordinary men show themselves a man, they change the world around them one person at a time. We can all ignite change.

Some of you like to start things. You are wired to build companies and plant churches. You are smart enough—and naive enough—to charge ahead and do bold things. You are the type who could whiteboard ideas all day. People tend to follow you, and you tend to follow your passions. If you are one of these men, go stir it up. What's the worst that could happen? What's the best that could happen?

Let's go stir it up.

CHAPTER 11

Endure

*Therefore, since we are surrounded by so great a cloud of witnesses,
let us also lay aside every weight, and sin which clings so closely, and
let us run with endurance the race that is set before us, looking to
Jesus, the founder and perfecter of our faith.*

—Heb. 12:1–2

I love meeting young men who claim they're tired and busy. I used
to be one of these guys, and I really did think I was tired and
busy. Catching me at the grocery store you'd ask, "How's it going,
man?" and I'd tell you I was busy. I wasn't faking; I really thought
I was. And coming from college, which is a fairy tale, I was busy,
relatively speaking.

Then I got a job, a wife, and children. Over time, I took on more
responsibility in business and church. My wife and I had another
child. I made time to write and exercise, further compressing the mar-
gin in my life.

Now I know what it means to be tired and busy. And I wish someone would have grabbed me by the shoulders back then and looked
in my dopey young eyes and explained what I was in for. I wish they

would have told me how wonderful it would be to have a life filled to the brim, a life so big it's impossible not to rely on God and praise him continuously. It would have been good to have set my mind right. If no one has given you that talk, allow me: you will be tired if you are living right.

If you have not yet experienced a full and meaningful life, let me tell you it is available. It is tiring, but it is worth it. What "busy" young men need to know is that they are going to be more tired and busier than they currently are and that it will never change—at least it won't change if they're doing it right.

We are here today and gone tomorrow. But we must play the long game, because God might give us a long life. With modern medicine, we will probably walk around on this earth for quite a while. So how do we keep on keeping on?

It can get tough out there, guys. Though a life lived under the kingship of Jesus is a good life, we will still fall on hard times. We will still struggle financially. Our sin will affect our loved ones and will spread its fever like a virus. We will be tempted and tried in this race, yet we must be strong and show ourselves as men. How can we do this?

One thing I rarely hear talked about is how to endure. There's plenty out there on how to lead your family, run a business, and get large triceps, but no one talks about the long grind of manhood—the uphill path that is hard but oh so worth it. We must talk about how to endure.

A MAN SHOULD BE TIRED

When you lay your head on your pillow at night, it should be a great relief. You should exhale and think, *Wow, what a day!* Showing yourself a man will require all of your resources mentally, physically, emotionally, and spiritually. You will be on empty at the end of most days.

You should be.

In our culture of comfort, exhaustion gets a bad rap. Sure, some overworked people neglect everything for work, but that's rare. And

I'm not talking about excessive busyness; that's just a symptom of a man out of control. To be moving at all times is either based in fear or disordered priorities. I am referring to good, hard work that makes a man get up early and spend himself. I am talking about being used up for good purposes.

The best men I know are exhausted when the sun goes down. They regroup, continuing to love and serve their families even while tired, and then get ready for the next day. This is a joyous routine, not a life of drudgery. Get up, work hard, serve, sleep, repeat. Smile.

We can experience burnout if we aren't careful, though. I find that when I think God depends upon me, I am inclined to work myself into the ground. Sometimes he lets me so that I become my own object lesson. Then as I lie there looking up at him, he smiles and picks me up. *Remember that I care for you, son. Remember that I hold all things together.*

Hard work is just that: it is hard and it is work. But it shouldn't break a man if his priorities are in line and his soul is refreshed in Jesus. That's the real difference. A soul refreshed in Jesus can flourish anywhere and at any time—sick and wounded or strong and healthy. To make sure our hard work is healthy, we must make sure our souls are healthy.

BE KIND TO YOURSELF

While you should be tired, if you run out of gas in the middle of the day or in the heat of the battle of life, it means you're doing something wrong. If you peter out early, you're not being more manly; you're probably neglecting yourself in some way.

I'm preaching to myself here. I am inclined to just get up earlier and push myself to work harder and get it all done. That is, until something breaks.

The other day my wife gently explained that I was becoming a complete jerk. I was doing a lot of writing in the early morning hours, but I was sleep deprived, though I felt fine. I would get up at 4:30 a.m., write for an hour, work out for an hour, and go to work. I'd get home and try to be helpful to Lindsay and the kids. I helped with the kids and preparing dinner, but all the while I gritted my teeth. I folded laundry spitefully because I didn't want to, or I washed dishes annoyed. A few times I lost my temper with the kids too easily. I really was being a jerk, and I didn't even know it. Apparently, sleep deprivation has that effect on me.

We are human. We need air to breathe and food to eat and water to drink, and we need sleep. Just because some of us can buckle down and get things done does not mean we should run hard all the time no matter the consequences. There are always consequences. This is a hard lesson to learn. Some men have clogged arteries and fat bellies. Stress has altered their lives. Others have distant relationships with their wives because work is their true love. Some men are just zombies who don't smile anymore, who don't interact with others. This is not a joyous life in Christ. It is missing what is offered to a man who walks in God's ways: deep joy and pleasure in our toil.

We must care for ourselves, men. Not only physically, as we talked about in chapter seven, though that is crucial. We must also care for our souls. We must treat ourselves with kindness.

This may sound vague or mystical to you. *I need to care for my soul? Come on, man. Really?* Yes, really. You are made up of mind, body, and soul. We have discussed ways to cultivate the mind, build the body, and engage the heart, which is the seat of the soul. When you love, you love from your soul. When you mourn, you mourn from your soul. When you pursue something creative or artistic, you do so from your soul. When you pray, you speak from your soul (hopefully). When you watch William Wallace rally his men to fight and it makes you want to grab the nearest sword and join them, that comes from your soul.

It's wrong thinking that causes us to burn out. This wrong thinking neglects our souls. Wrong thinking goes like this:

If I don't get this done . . .

> . . . it'll be late and what would they think of me?
> . . . I can't relax.

. . . I will fail miserably.

. . . it won't get done.

The secret to sane living is knowing that God's will is not contingent upon our performance. Rather, our performance is contingent upon God's will. Will he allow us to work hard? Will he provide the strength? He will save souls, feed the poor, and slay evil with or without you. We are dependent upon him, not him upon us.

If you take pride in telling people your work hours or how busy you are, you have a problem. If you haven't taken a vacation in years, you have a problem. If all of your hobbies and passions have died, you have a problem. If you don't laugh much anymore, you have a problem.

You probably have a problem.

We need rest, men. We need to sit still and let our souls breathe.

When we take our hands off the wheel that's steering our lives and rest, we learn that God has actually been driving all along. Rest is an act of trust. Rest acknowledges our weakness and God's strength. And it not only refreshes us, it builds more trust. It is a good cycle. We rest, God provides, and thus we are inclined to rest again.

God rested not because he was tired, but because it was healthy and he knew we needed to heed his example. I think God rested because he simply wanted to. I doubt his energy has limits. I think he rested because it gave him great joy.

SERIOUSLY, THOUGH, MAN UP

Never complain and never explain.
Benjamin Disraeli

Rest is crucial. We must trust God enough to sit down and be still. We must treat ourselves with the same love we're commanded to share with others.

But we still need to man up.

If we are to endure this long race of life, we need to toughen up. It is not showing yourself a man to complain and whimper when times get hard. Complaining is rooted in entitlement, and we must have a zero tolerance policy with whiny entitlement.

Let me tell you a story.

Australian explorer Douglas Mawson was thirty years old when he sailed to Antarctica in 1911. His goal: to map and explore some of the hardest places on the brutal continent. Once anchored in Commonwealth Bay, Mawson volunteered for the worst section:

> *Mawson's plan was to split his expedition into four groups, one to man base camp and the other three to head into the interior to do scientific work. He nominated himself to lead what was known as the Far Eastern Shore Party—a three-man team assigned to survey several glaciers hundreds of miles from base. It was an especially risky assignment. Mawson and his men have the furthest to travel, and hence the heaviest loads to carry, and they would have to cross an area pitted with deep crevasses, each concealed by snow.[1]*

Mawson chose the hardest route.

After nearly a year on the great white frozen continent, things were starting to go bad. And weird things were happening to the group, which sent a ripple of uneasiness through them. These strange happenings felt like bad omens. They found a female husky devouring her own puppies. Out of nowhere—remember, they're in the middle of nowhere—a bird slammed into their sled. Injuries started to compound. One of the members of their team, Bellgrave Ninnis, fell into a crevasse with his dogs and died. Mawson and the remaining member of their team called to Ninnis for hours, hoping he was just knocked unconscious. No answer ever came.

"May God help us," Mawson wrote in his diary.

They were out of food, so they killed and ate the weakest dog in their pack. As they headed back, they encountered a whiteout. Mawson became snow blind.

At this point Mawson's remaining companion was barely able to travel, but Mawson would not leave him. In bad shape himself, Mawson tended to the man. He even cleaned his companion after he lost control of his bowels. And then the man lost his mind. He died in the middle of the night.

Douglas Mawson continued on alone.

His feet and groin were raw meat. His nose and lips were split. He had no food, save for dog meat. Frostbite, blisters, and sores ravaged his body. Mawson wrote that his skin was peeling off his body. Too weak to walk, he dragged himself across the frozen surface.

Unbelievably, conditions got worse for Mawson. He fell into a crevasse, but the frayed rope he carried caught on an outcropping. He dangled between life and death. Mustering every last bit of resolve, he inched up the rope from which he hung, his hands slippery with blood from his raw hands. Miraculously, he made it out. He kept on.

Mawson finally made it back to base. A shore party who had been left behind to wait for him greeted him. Also there to greet him was the sight of the *Aurora*, the expedition ship, sailing away for Australia. Mawson had literally missed the boat. He would spend yet another winter in Antarctica recovering from his hellish trek.

Mending slowly, Mawson sent the following message to his fiancée:

> *Deeply regret delay. Only just managed to reach hut.*
> *Effects now gone but lost most of my hair. You are free*
> *to consider your contract but trust you will not abandon*
> *your second hand Douglas.*[2]

That's a *man*.

He had just endured a fate nearly worse than death, losing two of his friends and colleagues, and he had almost died himself. In what can only be described by what the Italians call *sprezzatura* (an attitude of artful nonchalance), Mawson casually apologizes for being late and jokes about his fiancée reconsidering their engagement since he has lost most of his hair in his journey. He did not whimper or complain; he laughed it off and moved forward.

It is highly doubtful that any of us will experience a harrowing journey like that of Douglas Mawson. You would literally have to try to make all of that happen. But we will face difficult trials. Our children will stray and our loved ones will die. Our bodies will break down and our minds will, too. We will be betrayed. We may get fired from our jobs. This broken world will blindside us. Life is no cake walk.

How will we respond? You have a choice, you know. Like Mawson, you can either trust God, press on, and drag yourself along; or you can give up and quit. You can complain, or you can laugh it off in a self-deprecating joke. You can remain faithful, or you can give in to hopelessness. You do not choose your circumstances, but you do choose your reaction to them.

In his article entitled "Never Complain; Never Explain," Brett McKay states, "The world doesn't exist to meet my expectations, and if they're not met, I figure I can do one of two things—go somewhere else, or create something myself more to my liking."[3]

God has given us great freedom to make decisions. In the quest of forging our manhood, one of the very first decisions we should make is never complain, never whine, and never let entitlement creep in.

DON'T GET TAKEN OUT

I heard a story the other day of a godly man who was taken out. He is a good man who loves Jesus, loves his family, and treats others with respect and love. This man, whom we'll call Dave, was the head of a multimillion dollar company. He had the corner office.

Dave's company hired a young woman to join their team, and because Dave was one of the most senior leaders, he offered to take her around to their operations. He also offered to train her.

Normally an open-door guy with people coming in and out of his office all day, Dave decided to shut the door for his training meetings with the young woman. It gave them uninterrupted time to talk. He drove her to the different operations. The young woman got up to speed quickly. All was going well.

That is, until the accusation.

Two of his close friends at the company accused Dave of having an affair with the woman. They told him, condescendingly, they were "praying" for him. The entire office caught wind of the rumor. Dave tried to make it all go away by gathering everyone together and clearing the air, but the damage was done. He was stripped of his position and humiliated. His reputation was trashed.

Dave was taken out, even though he had not been unfaithful to his wife or unprofessional with the young woman.

Satan is in the business of taking good men out. He is cunning and has millennia of experience in tempting men. He picked off Dave. He will do the same to you and me if given an opportunity. It could be an allegation of an affair, or we may actually give in to infidelity. We might slowly build the habit of drinking ourselves unconscious. We may, in the search for release from stress, look to harmful alternatives in the search for peace, which only comes from Christ. Or maybe we'll just become hard. In each of these situations, Satan takes us out.

I don't think we are aware when this is happening. I don't think we understand that we are across the wire, downrange, in enemy territory. All seems quiet and safe. But the Devil prowls like a lion seeking someone to devour. You and I are the prey. Watch your back. Pay close attention to yourself and the voices you listen to. Stay close to Scripture and wise counsel. Do not isolate yourself, for an isolated man is easy prey.

Satan has set countless snares, and some of them are crafty and camouflaged. If we are to endure the long haul, we must watch our steps. For example, Dave should have been more careful with having so much one-on-one time with the young woman. He should have kept his office door open. These small but significant safeguards may have avoided the rumors and accusations. He learned this lesson in a very hard way. Hindsight is 20/20. Being hypervigilant in our lives isn't paranoia; its situational awareness. The snares that are the most dangerous are the ones tied to something inherently good, which is generally the case.

The bait sounds like these internal messages (note the good things the snares are tied to):

> *You aren't doing enough.* (Good thing: Work)
>
> *Of course you're lusting. Your wife is holding out on you.* (Good thing: Intimacy)
>
> *Have another; you've earned it.* (Good thing: Feasting and Enjoyment)
>
> *Quote that verse to show them how much you know.* (Good thing: Scripture)

These messages are designed to lead you toward sin and destruction. They are designed to take a good thing and twist it into a bad thing. This is Satan's MO. His snares are surreptitious; they come in like a wolf in sheep's clothing.

If we resort to passivity or obliviousness, we'll wake up miles down the wrong road. We'll get taken out.

While we all must be careful to be on guard against the wiles of the Devil, the more successful we are, the more danger we're in. Success usually comes with money, prestige, and power. With money you can prop yourself up in a lie of a lifestyle. Prestige can usher in pride. Power can be an avenue to oppress those under your authority. But eventually, if your life is built on the shifting sands of your own ideas, it will all come crashing down on top of you. If you have forsaken your love for Jesus for a different love (power, money, sex, etc.), you are caught in Satan's snare. It will likely be painful to get free from its grasp, but the good news is that you can get free.

We are not alone. The Lord goes with us as we travel through life. He protects us from untold amounts of evil and temptation. He does not evaluate your value like Santa Claus with a list of your good and bad deeds. Jesus demonstrated exactly what he thinks of you as his blood pooled beneath the cross. His love for you cost him his life. He is strong and victorious, and he will keep you from all kinds of evil.

But you are still in enemy territory. Look alive. Stay awake. Be vigilant over your life.

THE WELL

If we want to finish well in the race of life, we need sustenance to help us endure. Runners need water or they will lose strength and overheat. This is especially true for long runs in enemy territory.

I have found that when I neglect to read Scripture and pray, I become lost. It is not merely that I have broken a good habit; something supernatural happens to me. I get tired more easily. I am more irritable. I lose perspective.

We are not inherently good men. Sorry if that's a surprise to you. If we were inherently good men, we could be our own guiding light. You know, *follow your heart*. That sounds really good on paper, but if you follow your heart, as determined by your momentary desires— you'll end up out of gas and out of your mind.

When Jesus met the Samaritan woman at the well, he turned her life upside down. She came to the well just to fill her water container, but she received far more than that. A Jewish man and a Samaritan woman were not supposed to hang out at the watering hole together. It was uncouth. But Jesus didn't care. He stepped right in.

Let's catch them in mid conversation:

> *Jesus answered her, "If you knew the gift of God, and who it is that is saying to you, 'Give me a drink,' you would have asked him, and he would have given you living water." The woman said to him, "Sir, you have nothing to draw water with, and the well is deep. Where do you get that living water? Are you greater than our father Jacob? He gave us the well and drank from it himself, as did his sons and his*

livestock." Jesus said to her, "Everyone who drinks of this water will be thirsty again, but whoever drinks of the water that I will give him will never be thirsty again. The water that I will give him will become in him a spring of water welling up to eternal life." The woman said to him, "Sir, give me this water, so that I will not be thirsty or have to come here to draw water."

John 4:10–15

The Samaritan woman had a jug with which to draw water, but Jesus had none. Breaking cultural convention, he asked for a drink. She is astounded by Jesus. She has no idea who he is.

Jesus explained that it is he who can provide the real water—the water of eternal life. Though she had the ability to draw from the well, Jesus had the power to draw from the well of grace. The water he provides—that is, himself—is a spring of water that wells up into eternal life. If one had to choose, Jesus's water is clearly the superior choice. And he offered this water to her. After some conversation in which Jesus dazzled the Samaritan woman with his knowledge of her life, she ran off. She was changed. She left her water jar sitting by the well and hurried to the next town. She told the townspeople: "Come, see a man who told me all that I ever did" (v. 29).

The Samaritan woman came to the well for water and went away having met the Living Water himself. He peered into her soul. She had found the well.

Many of us play the short game with life. We think of our lives in terms of today and tomorrow. In a sense, this is good. It is biblical, even—when kept in balance. But we should think of our endurance in terms of the long game. Wisdom takes time. Sanctification is a slow process. My point is we need to prepare for the journey. We need to visit the well daily to make sure our soul is filled up with Jesus as we live the adventure of each day.

Jesus knew something about long journeys, about endurance. Consider the distance he traveled on foot:

> *Jesus, like many of his contemporaries, crisscrossed the country numerous times. Assuming he went from Nazareth to Jerusalem annually for each of the three required annual feasts using the shortest route through Samaria, a distance of 75 miles each way, he would have walked a minimum of 13,500 miles before beginning his ministry. On at least one of his later pilgrimages, he went from Capernaum to Jerusalem by way of Jericho, 106 miles each way. Estimating conservatively, Jesus probably walked at least 15,000 miles in his lifetime.[4]*

Jesus's journeys were hard and often stressful. At times he traveled alone, and sometimes others journeyed with him. Other times his traveling partners were amicable and helpful; other times they bickered like spoiled children, making his life miserable. He took each day as it came and endured. Sounds a bit like our lives, doesn't it?

Moments of spiritual ecstasy are rare on the path with Jesus. I've had some pretty phenomenal moments in my walk with God, but most phenomenal is the grace in a million ordinary moments. If we try to ride the tide of the highs, we'll run aground when the tide recedes. We need a perspective of endurance. We must patiently press toward Jesus, who is himself the prize of heaven. How will we do this? Where exactly is the well found?

The well is found . . .

    . . . in your Bible.

    . . . in your church family.

    . . . in the counsel of the wise brothers to your left and right.

    . . . in prayer.

    . . . in solitude.

The wellhead is always Jesus. So it is in these things above that we must seek him. These are just the means. For example, if we read the Bible to get knowledge, we will remain thirsty. If we go to church only to make new friends, we will remain thirsty. But if we approach the Bible and church family as the means to the wellhead of Christ, we'll drink deeply.

Drink deeply of the well. If you do, you can endure anything.

CHAPTER 12

Die Hard

*Our glorious Leader never squanders the lives of his soldiers; he
values the church militant beyond all price; and though he permits
his saints to lay down their lives for his sake, yet is not one life spent
in vain, or unnecessarily expended.*

—Charles Spurgeon

While our paths differ, our journeys lead us home to the same place. We must all pass through the gate of death. We are moving ever toward this gate, the unavoidable chasm. It is our last transition point into another world. You might not put this on a coffee cup, but that is where we are headed. It does not matter how you live. It does not matter if you stuff death down into the category of *it won't happen to me*. It's coming, and it's coming sooner than later.

I say bring it on.

Living a full-hearted life means death doesn't threaten to create a long list of "could-have-beens." If we courageously pursue that which God calls us toward right now, we will have few regrets to sort through on our deathbeds. The Christian life begins by the death of self and ends with the death of self; then it begins anew in the land of perfection.

To the Christian, death is not an end—it's a transition, and a glorious one at that. Death brings us to the waiting arms of Christ. What could there be to fear? Dietrich Bonhoeffer said it well: "When Christ calls a man, he bids him come and die."[1]

Death is not the real killer of life. Fear is. Death is such a knee-buckling topic because too many of us fear death. But why? What can we do about it? Did we really think we'd live forever on this earth in these bodies? None have, and none ever will. Death is inevitable and unpredictable. We can prop people up with medicines and machines for quite a long time, but eventually we cannot sustain them.

Fear drives a man to desert his brothers in the middle of battle. Fear makes parents coddle the life out of their kids. Fear keeps hopes and dreams locked away. Fear handcuffs men and keeps them from pursuing their calling. It is deadly. It is worse than death.

SCARS

Scars are beautiful. They are the marks of travel, pain, and effort. The weathered old man is a sight to behold, as he has lived long and seen much. Wherever the paths of life have taken him, he has lived under the reign of God for many years. His mistakes scarred him, but they have also taught him. He may not recognize it, but when he lived contrary to God's design, he brought pain and suffering upon himself. When he lived in harmony with God's design, he flourished. He wears the marks of time and truth.

As death approaches, it should inspire us to live. We cannot avoid death, but we can avoid life. If we don't live ferociously, on full blast, we may find that our lives haven't amounted to much. But if we grasp our future beyond the grave, our approaching deaths should remove our fears. It is coming anyway, so we might as well live. May we live hard and bright and full, as God allows. Our time is a gift to enjoy with Jesus as we glorify him.

Last Christmas we unwrapped presents and left the trash on the floor. Given that we are blessed to be able to provide generously for our kids, we made a lot of trash. As our kids unwrapped their presents, they not only delighted in the gifts, but they rooted around in the trash, giggling like mad. They were happy little maniacs. We should live like this, unwrapping the gift of each day and playing in what it brings. We have a good Father who has given us many gifts.

Live hard; die hard.

PERSPECTIVE FOR LIVING

If you are troubled by a decision, think about the choice you'll value most on your deathbed. For example, will you wish you had more quality time with your family, or will you wish you had more money? Would you rather have had an impressive title at work, or kids that really know you? What will matter as you draw your last breaths? Most decisions, even small ones, can be framed this way.

I call this *deathbed perspective*. Deathbed perspective is living life in view of death. That may sound morbid, but it's anything but. Death-bed perspective can make you fully alive. If you understand that your time is finite, you'll treat it with respect. You will be sure to tell your loved ones how you feel about them. You will use your time wisely regarding work and creative endeavors. If you remember that your life is short, you will be much less inclined to waste time.

We feel this at funerals, don't we? While we mourn for the person we've lost, we also mourn the shortness of time. It hangs heavy in the air like an invisible cloak. Sitting in the pews dressed in our finery, we can't help but think, *I am going to die.* Death is unnerving and thus hurts those left behind. But it also pulls back the curtain for them and helps them remember that earth is not our forever home. God turns the darkness of death into his glorious light as he welcomes his children home and comforts those left behind.

The wisdom of old age is a combination of lessons learned and perspective gained through a lifetime. When we are old, we cannot fool ourselves into thinking we'll live forever. We start counting years.

Do not let old age or the nearness of death rob you of life. Grab a hold of the fear of death and flip it upside down. Remember what happened when Jesus ascended after his death? He not only proved he was exactly who he said he was, he also purchased eternity for all of us. Death isn't so scary when it gets into the ring with Jesus. He annihilated death.

Let your short life remind you to live a faithful and fearless life.

WE NEED YOU

As men age, they season. After a long while of aging, the gap between an old man and a young man widens. The two are from different worlds. For example, kids today intuitively use technology as a normal part of their lives, but for the elderly, technology is confusing wizardry. Different worlds.

These different worlds are only different scenes of God's story. It's still the same narrative with the same arc and the same wonderful ending. If you have read the Bible much at all, you know there are no new problems, only new manifestations of age-old ones. Old men who have walked in the ways of God and have shown themselves a man know God's story well. Instead of putting sages out to pasture, we need to seat them in an honored place, pull up a chair, and learn from them. We need the men ahead of us in the race to tell us what they've seen. *Slow down around this turn, young man; it's a doozie.*

If you are a young man, seek an older man's counsel. If you are an older man, make yourself available to young men. Young men are full of swagger, and many of them think they know everything, but you older men know well and good that they don't. They need you. We need you. Please don't stop trying to make the world a better place. Please don't stop telling people about Jesus. Don't stop until it's your time to leave. We need you.

It is sad when an old man loses the fire in his belly. This usually happens when he thinks he's lost his usefulness to the world. God created men to be useful, and when a man ceases to be useful, even if only his own eyes, despair sets in. Wisdom has no expiration date, though. As we grow old in the race of life, may we befriend younger men and show them along.

A LEGACY FOR OTHERS

Having shown yourself a man, when you are gone, your story of who you were remains. It will be passed around at family gatherings and drinks between friends. If you have lived a cowardly life, no one will talk much about what you could have done; you will quickly be forgotten. If you have lived a bold life, there's probably more to talk about. Even better, if you have lived a bold and *godly* life, books could be written of your story. But that isn't the point.

As we think about our legacy, about what we will leave behind, we should consider what truly matters. It is wonderful to leave an inheritance, and some are blessed to do so. But what really matters, what changes history, even eternity, is a story of a life well lived. That is why we love biographies. It is why we love stories. Stories help us frame our reality.

The Bible is not a random collection of short stories and letters penned by ancient sages. It is a multifaceted story of God's redemptive plan for us. That story is still being written. And just who is the hero of God's story? Jesus. Thus, our legacy should be about the hero (note that we are not the hero).

When Pappaw, my father's father, passed away, I was too young to know him. But his legacy lives on. I see his face in my dad, my uncle, and my aunt. I hear stories of his lighthearted humor, how he'd slowly enjoy a cigarette and cup of coffee on the way to the office instead of hurrying like most of us do. My dad tells me how much Pappaw loved his wife, Mammaw. We have a black-and-white picture of the two of them standing in a yard somewhere looking like movie stars. I see Dad's eyes change when he talks about them. Pappaw lived to be only in his fifties, but his legacy lives on. He still impacts our lives today, and I am who I am in part because of a man I never really met.

That's the power of a legacy.

What if we really understood this? What if we understood that the quality of our lives will frame the understanding of those who come after us? Here is what you must understand: *your legacy is for others.*

You'll be dead and gone while others live on. They will pick up what you left behind. What will you leave them? Too many of us think about our legacy in purely selfish terms. We want people to think well of us, and we want to preserve a certain image. We fight to protect that image at all costs. But our reputations are not for us; we won't even be here. Our legacy is about glorifying God and shining that glory into the lives of our fellow travelers. As God's children and ambassadors in the world, we reflect him to others. In our increasingly secular world, you may be the only glimpse of Jesus someone sees. Will you reflect him well? Will your legacy tell his story?

When a man walks in God's ways over a lifetime, he *shows himself a man*. He will stumble and fall, but he keeps going toward the prize of heaven. He serves others and pushes back the darkness. He builds businesses and creates an environment that helps others flourish. He volunteers to fight Goliath when everyone else shrinks back. He enjoys a cup of coffee and stops to watch the sun rise. He smiles inside as he feels the warmth of his Father's breath upon him. He rises, he opens his mouth, and he opens his life.

He changes the world because of God's change in him.

Acknowledgments

To each person who reads my work or supports me in any way, thank you for giving me a platform to say what's on my heart and mind. Writing a book is a solitary effort, but it is much easier to write when you know people have your back. Those of you who support me make it possible for me to write. I am grateful.

I want to first thank the man who showed me what true manhood looks like. Dad, I admire and respect you. I look up to you and hope to honor you as long as God gives me life. Lindsay, my love, thank you for putting up with me during the frenzy of getting this book done. I could not have done it without you. Mom, you are unflinching in your love and support. No matter what is going on in your life, you lay it aside to be there for others. Thank you for supporting my writing. To Uncle Don, thank you for your example, your love, and our adventures together. You have shown me what it looks like to be a man who is present in the moment. Bob, you are an inspiration to me as a man. You have an intense work ethic and a deep love for your family. Your kind and gentle ways encourage me, and you always get behind my projects to hold me up. To Nick, my wingman. We hung tight together during some very formative years, and your friendship is dear to my heart. I hope to build more fenced-in areas soon. Casey, our bond as siblings runs deep. Thank you for having my back and for being my big sister. To Diana, thank you for standing by another of my harebrained projects. You are a great source of strength in my life. Neathery, thank you for your work on this project. You made it beautiful, not only visually, but you helped to cast the vision for what this book could become. I am honored to be on the creative journey with you and I look forward to our mutual instigation of big things. To Erin Brown, my editor, thank you for polishing my words. The readers may never know you, but they will be blessed by your work. To Elliott, you define what it means to be a true friend. I thank God for the gift of being your friend and brother. To Scott, Keith, Bob, Steve, and the entire body of The Door Church, thank you for your love of Christ and your spiritual care for me. Thank you for being a healthy, spiritual family focused on the glory of Christ.

To my Kickstarter supporters, you made this project happen. Thank you for believing in this book.

Sometimes God sets you on a path leading to the unknown. He just says, "Go." A decade ago he set me on a path to write this book, though I was not aware of the particulars. It started and stopped—mostly stopped. But God was fathering me and preparing me to write this book. He was preparing me to open my mouth about the powerful topic of manhood. To say I am thankful for his work in my life is an understatement, as my life is completely in his hands. I pray that he is glorified by this book.

Notes

Introduction

1. CCAP, "The Disappearing College Male," Forbes, May 4, 2015, https://www.forbes.com/sites/ccap/2015/05/04/the-disappearing-college-male/#7b73e1244d3c.

2. Rich Morin, "The Disappearing Male Worker," Pew Research Center, September 3, 2013, http://www.pewresearch.org/fact-tank/2013/09/03/the-disappearing-male-worker/.

3. Sally C. Curtin, MA, Margaret Warner, PhD, and Holly Hedegaard, MD, MSPH, "Increase in Suicide in the United States, 1999–2014," Centers for Disease Control and Prevention, NCHS Data Brief No. 241, April 2016, https://www.cdc.gov/nchs/products/databriefs/db241.htm.

4. Charles E. Blue, "Testosterone Levels in Men Decline Over Past Two Decades, Study Shows," Endocrine Society, https://www.endocrine.org/news-room/press-release-archives/2006/testosterone_lvls_in_men_decline.

Chapter 1

1. Jennifer Homans, "A Woman's Place: *The End of Men*, by Hanna Rosin," *New York Times*, September 13, 2012, http://www.nytimes.com/2012/09/16/books/review/the-end-of-men-by-hanna-rosin.html.

2. Barna Group, "The End of Absolutes: America's New Moral Code," May 25, 2016, https://www.barna.com/research/the-end-of-absolutes-americas-new-moral-code/.

3. "Gender & Gender Identity," Planned Parenthood, https://www.plannedparenthood.org/learn/sexual-orientation-gender/gender-

gender-identity.

4. Paul David Tripp, *What Did You Expect?: Redeeming the Realities of Marriage* (Illinois: Crossway, 2010), 67.

5. "How Did Britain Let 250,000 Underage Soldiers Fight in WW1?" BBC, http://www.bbc.co.uk/guides/zcvdhyc.

6. "Solving the Mystery of Rudyard Kipling's Son," *BBC*, January 18, 2016, http://www.bbc.com/news/magazine-35321716.

7. "WW1 Casualties," WWI Facts, http://ww1facts.net/quick-reference/ww1-casualties/.

8. Lee Dye, "Why Are More Men Waiting to Marry?" *ABC News*, August 14, 2014, http://abcnews.go.com/Technology/story?id=97920&page=1.

9. Alfred E. Kahn, "The Tyranny of Small Decisions: Market Failures, Imperfections, and the Limits of Economics," 1966, *International Review for Social Sciences*, http://onlinelibrary.wiley.com/doi/10.1111/j.1467-6435.1966.tb02491.x/pdf.

10. John Eldredge, *Wild at Heart: Discovering the Secret of a Man's Soul* (Nashville: Thomas Nelson, 2001), 9.

Chapter 2

1. Stephen Mansfield, *Mansfield's Book of Manly Men: An Utterly Invigorating Guide to Being Your Most Masculine Self* (Nashville: Thomas Nelson, 2013), 34.

Chapter 3

1. "Pornography Statistics: 2015 Report," Covenant Eyes, http://www.covenanteyes.com/pornstats/.

2. Tim Worstall, "Astonishing Numbers: America's Poor Still Live Better Than Most of The Rest of Humanity," Forbes, June 1, 2013, https://www.forbes.com/sites/timworstall/2013/06/01astonishi

ng-numbers-americas-poor-still-live-better-than-most-of-the-
rest-of-humanity/2/#3d4046ef7b4f.

3. Theodore Roosevelt, *The Strenuous Life: Essays and Addresses*, 2015,
   Kindle ed.

Chapter 4

1. C. S. Lewis, *Mere Christianity* (New York: Touchstone, 1996), 56.

Chapter 5

1. Needtobreathe, "Wasteland."

Chapter 6

1. Fyodor Dostoyevsky, *The Brothers Karamazov* (New York: Dover,
   2005), 94.

2. Amy Craft, "Books vs. e-books: The Science behind the Best Way
   to Read," *CBS News*, December 14, 2015, http://www.cbsnews.
   com/news/kindle-nook-e-reader-books-the-best-way-to-read/.

3. John Coleman, "For Those Who Want to Lead, Read," *Harvard
   Business Review*, August 15, 2012, https://hbr.org/2012/08/for-
   those-who-want-to-lead-rea.

4. C. S. Lewis, "Is Theology Poetry?" in Augustine Collective, http://
   augustinecollective.org/wp-content/uploads/2016/06/1.2-Is-
   Theology-Poetry-Reading.pdf.

5. Ibid.

6. Thrice, "Digital Sea," *The Alchemy Index* Vols. I & II (Vagrant
   Records, 2007).

7. Billy Graham, interview by Sarah Pulliam Bailey, "Q & A: Billy
   Graham on Aging, Regrets, and Evangelicals," *Christianity Today*,

January 21, 2011, http://www.christianitytoday.com/ct/2011/januaryweb-only/qabillygraham.html?start=2.

Chapter 7

1. National Institute of Diabetes and Digestive and Kidney Diseases, "Overweight and Obesity Statistics," https://www.niddk.nih.gov/health-information/health-statistics/overweight-obesity.

2. Gary Foster, in Alex O'Meara, "The Percentage of People Who Regain Weight after Rapid Weight Loss and the Risks of Doing So," LiveStrong.com, updated November 7, 2015, http://www.livestrong.com/article/438395-the-percentage-of-people-who-regain-weight-after-rapid-weight-loss-risks/.

Chapter 8

1. John Muir, *The Yosemite* (New York: The Century Co., 1912), 256.

Chapter 9

1. John Piper, "Christ: The Lion and the Lamb" (sermon, March 23, 1986), Desiring God, http://www.desiringgod.org/messages/christ-the-lion-and-the-lamb.

Chapter 10

1. Eric Gritsch, "1517 Luther Posts the 95 Theses," *Christianity Today*, Issue 28, http://www.christianitytoday.com/history/issues/issue-28/1517-luther-posts-95-theses.html, and Martin Luther Biography, Biography.com, http://www.biography.com/people/martin-luther-9389283.

2. Stephen Mansfield, *Mansfield's Book of Manly Men*, 25–28.

3. Blake Mycoskie, "How I Did It: The TOMS Story," *Entrepreneur*, September 20, 2011, https://www.entrepreneur.com/article/220350.

4. Shana Lebowitz, "On the 10th anniversary of TOMS, its founder talks stepping down, bringing in private equity, and why giving away shoes provides a competitive advantage," *Business Insider*, June 2016, http://www.businessinsider.com/toms-blake-mycoskie-talks-growing-a-business-while-balancing-profit-with-purpose-2016-6.

Chapter 11

1. Mike Dash, "The Most Terrible Polar Exploration Ever: Douglas Mawson's Antarctic Journey," *Smithsonian*, January 27, 2012, http://www.smithsonianmag.com/history/the-most-terrible-polar-exploration-ever-douglas-mawsons-antarctic-journey-82192685/.

2. Douglas Mawson, in David Killick, "Life and Death in the Home of the Blizzard," *Australian Antarctic Magazine*, Issue 22: Mawson Centenary Special, 2012, http://www.antarctica.gov.au/magazine/2011-2015/issue-22-2012/exploration/life-and-death-in-the-home-of-the-blizzard.

3. Brett McKay and Kate McKay, "Never Complain; Never Explain," The Art of Manliness, February 9, 2016, http://www.artofmanliness.com/2016/02/09/never-complain-never-explain/.

4. Merilyn Hargis, "On the Road," *Christianity Today*, Issue 59, http://www.christianitytoday.com/history/issues/issue-59/on-road.html.

Chapter 12

1. Dietrich Bonhoeffer, *The Cost of Discipleship* (New York: Touchstone, 1959), 89.

About the Author

BRAD LARSON is an author and entrepreneur. His first book, *Walking Through Walls: Connecting Faith and Work,* was published in late 2015. Brad is the host of *The Manifesto Podcast,* which is aimed at helping men live bold lives under the kingship of Jesus. When he's not chasing his kids, training jiu-jitsu, working out, or trying to grow a business, he writes. (That means he gets up really early and drinks a lot of coffee.)

You can find out more about Brad at *bradleydlarson.com.*